T0089699

Your Soul
Purpose

Your Soul Purpose

Learn How to Access the Light Within

Kim Russo

HarperOne
An Imprint of HarperCollinsPublishers

HarperOne

Chakra Body, Vibrational Charts, and Numerology Chart
created and designed by Joseph Russo, Graphic Designer. 2018.

Astrology Chart
Moj0jo/Shutterstock.com

Metatron Cube
elfinadesign/Shutterstock.com

Flower of Life
elfinadesign/Shutterstock.com

Feng Shui Bagua
Peter Hermes Furian/Shutterstock.com

Kabbalah/Flower of Life
Anne Mathiasz/Shutterstock.com

HarperCollins books may be purchased for educational, business, or sales promotional use. For information, please email the Special Markets Department at SPsales@harpercollins.com.

FIRST HARPERCOLLINS PAPERBACK EDITION PUBLISHED IN 2020

Library of Congress Cataloging-in-Publication Data is available upon request.

ISBN 978-0-06-285486-5

23 24 25 26 27 LBC 8 7 6 5 4

There Really Is Something About Mary

My Dearest Mary:

I can't believe the day has come, we had to say goodbye;
We stood beside you hopelessly and tried so not to cry

When we were kids you took the lead among our little crowd;
You guided us and mothered us and were always very proud

You talked us up and made a fuss, you bragged relentlessly;
With pride and joy, and eyes so wide, you loved your family

What will we do? Who will we ask the answers we don't know?
Who will promote and cheer us on when putting on our shows?

You cared so much about us all and put yourself as last;
You laughed so hard until you cried as you spoke about our past

Your name is very special, as our Mother up above;
Your name is filled with faith and hope, but most of all just love

I know you hear us when we cry and try to ease our pain;
We know you had a job to do and didn't die in vain

You always knew the things to say to make us feel at ease;
But now you're gone and we are lost, and trying not to grieve

The fun we had, the things we did as cousins till the end;
What made our bond was not just blood, we were each other's friend

Until we meet again, my dearest Mary—save a spot for me right next
   to you.
You are always in my heart,

                                    Kim Ellen (as only you would call me)

"There are two great days in a person's life—the day we are born and the day we discover why."

—WILLIAM BARCLAY

Contents

Introduction

Dear Reader,

Thank you for picking up *Your Soul Purpose*! As you read through these pages you might wonder if this book really can answer the questions you have. Will they point you in the right direction to find your own truth and the peace within that truth? Because I only deal with truths—something that often scares us—you might already be contemplating whether or not you should continue reading. Let me say this: If you have gotten this far in your thinking, this far on the page, then the answer is *yes! Go for it!*

Like many people alive on Earth today, you may be wondering What is this life all about? For what purpose was I born? Am I really who I think I am? Am I really who others think I am? If you believe in reincarnation (and I'll explain that in the book) you might be wondering if you're here to suffer through the lessons you didn't learn in a previous life. Maybe you're worried you had previously slanted toward evil and now it's payback time. I can hear you asking if your purpose is really to wake up every weekday at 5 a.m. to catch a crowded train, or sit in backed-up traffic, only to get to a job where no one even notices your accomplishments. There are many of you who are wondering when your current job will be taken over by a computer software program. (Hint: That may be sooner than you think.) And there are the voices of so many of you in my ear, who are reevaluating the relationships in your life that don't seem to be serving your highest good or highest purpose. These relationships pull energy from you and from your soul, leaving you empty and wrung-out like a used dishrag. You are continually searching for ways to escape these relationships, but the lies creep in and convince you that you made your bed and now you must lie in it. The only word in that sentence that is true is the lie.

If any of the above applies to you, then keep on reading!

You may have done a bit of soul-searching online already. Or maybe you went to a bookstore or to the library and worked your way through nonfiction, religious, and spiritual books, all the way to *Your Soul Purpose.* Some of you may have selected this book simply because you are familiar with *The Haunting of . . . ,* the TV show where I help celebrities solve the mysteries surrounding their otherworldly experiences. If so, then you already know me, my face, my Long Island accent—and you know I don't mess around. I have to tell it like it is! Others of you may have read my first book, *The Happy Medium: Life Lessons from the Other Side.* In those pages I told my personal story of finding, accepting, and understanding the spiritual gifts that have led me to discover my soul purpose.

In *The Happy Medium,* I also shared stories of how I met and got to know my many spiritual teachers. These teachers range from Kali, my husband's spirit guide, whom I stumbled into by accident, to a woman I met by chance (or not!), Holly, who stalked me until I stopped to listen to the many truths she was offering to share with me. One of the things I came to know through Holly was that no matter what your faith, following, beliefs, or disbeliefs, the spiritual world exists outside these distinctions, transcends them, and can peacefully coexist with them. These messengers, and many others I've met over the past 20-plus years, have imparted valuable wisdom that they've collected since the beginning of time. They have helped me to better understand the mysteries of The Universe and the seemingly unknowable; they've uncovered answers to questions I'd been asking since before I could even form words.

I consider these wise teachers, here on Earth as well as in the spirit world, to be the gurus who have shown up for me when I, the student, was ready to open my heart and receive the wisdom of their teachings. As is expected, there have been some ideas thrown at me that did not resonate with my soul. In those cases, I took what I needed and left the rest. My goal in writing this book is not to convince you of anything, and not to be your personal guru. My goal is to help you find the *guru that resides inside each and every one of you.* So, as I do when I'm receiving lessons, take what you need and leave what doesn't work for you.

In *Your Soul Purpose*, I'll walk you through the steps necessary to get to know yourself and to get to know God through yourself. I'll help you identify your passion, which is your purpose, so that you can live a life honoring that passion and gift. And I'll tell you about a new spirit guide who recently showed up when I least expected. He's the one who's helping me write this book and he told me about the major paradigm shifts occurring in the world today. There are many more details on that in the final chapter of this book.

Whether you're a celebrity, a stay-at-home mom or dad, a construction worker, a surgeon, a librarian, a physics professor, a college student, or anything in between: *You are holding the very book designed to help you.* No matter what your profession, level of education, level of wealth, religion, or country of origin, you and I and all the other readers are essentially alike. We are one and the same in our needs and desires.

Like Dorothy in *The Wizard of Oz*, each one of us yearns to find our way "home," the place where we are loved and feel safe. We're usually not sure where that place is or how to get there. We pick up friends along the way, people with brains, courage, and heart. These people are searching too; together we wander down the yellow brick road of life. Of course, there are good witches and bad witches. And let's not forget those crazy-eyed flying monkeys who scare the heck outta us on this journey! The world has an endless number of external barriers trying to distract us on our way home. What we fail to realize during this seemingly treacherous journey is that we don't need to take that yellow brick road at all. We don't need to wander so far. The answer, the home we're looking for, is nesting inside each of us, pulsing with energy and purpose. And this purpose, this passion, is what we are supposed to do with our lives. That, along with the other details of your life, is written on what I call the Master Blueprint.

Naturally, you're wondering where this blueprint is and why you don't have access to it. Well, you do! The blueprint is held by a Higher

Intelligence and creator of all things. We are all sparks of this *Divine Energy*, also known as *Love* (first and foremost), *The God Force*, *The Omnipresent One*, *The Universe*, *Your Higher Self*, *Higher Power*, *Infinite Wisdom*, *Divine Mind*, *Higher Intelligence*, *The Light*, *Spirit*, *The I Am*, or *Source*. The most popular name, and what most people call this energy, is *God*. You will see these titles referred to interchangeably throughout this book. The God Force is all-encompassing, and is a Supreme Energy Source. God is neither male nor female; therefore, to make things simpler, I will use the pronouns *He* and *Him* when referring to God. Whatever you choose to call it, it is connected to each one of us. Our infinite connection to this energy is our birthright. It is contained in our DNA like wires or microchips in a computer's hard drive. Just like the wireless internet, by using the right side of our brains, and through our hearts, we are able to make an instant connection to this energy. It is always available, remembers what you forgot when you were born, and transcends logic, time, and space.

Remember Dorothy finding her way to the Wizard, only to find out the Wizard held no power to help her? It turned out that the only way home was through herself. It was information she already knew but had to be reminded of: *There's no place like home, there's no place like home* . . . (It amazes me how enlightened L. Frank Baum was. I might have to find his spirit, so we can further discuss the Oz books and the movie.)

When you use the blueprint and work in tandem with the divine knowledge of The Higher Power, you can evolve individually while also contributing to the elevation of *all* of humanity. Together on this journey, we can hammer away at the walls that separate us through judgment and fear. These twin forces are the driving emotions behind hate, war, and all the negativity that corrupts humanity. With faith, courage, and the knowledge of The Higher Power, we can collectively move toward peace, compassion, and love.

Throughout this book, I will help you understand who you truly are and why you are meant to be here at this very tumultuous yet wondrous time on the planet. I will blow open the lid on the many lies that were taught to you at an early age by authority figures. These were lies that often led you to feeling hopeless, helpless, and confused.

Like holding a map to a treasure chest, this book will lead you across the terrain of your life, to the discovery of your soul purpose, your passion. You'll learn the spiritual truths about your soul, the spiritual laws that govern your soul, and much, much more.

I am a soul who has decided to incarnate—to join a body—at this particular time in history. My purpose is to demonstrate the highest and purest expression of my unique soul energy; to learn, teach, create, and love. Your purpose is connected to my purpose. I am so grateful that you are allowing me into your life to deliver the tools you need to find the answers you are seeking.

Before we get started, find a highlighter pen and a cozy nook where you can settle in. Take off your shoes, take off your tie, and take off any resistance or hesitations you might be grasping onto. Try to release the awareness you have of your body or the room you're in, or the room you're not in. (Forget about those shoes scattered across the floor, or the stacks of things "to go upstairs" sitting on your stairs.) Pretend you have just landed here from another planet and have no expectations or ideas of how life works on Earth. Pretend you've never learned any of the things that limit, restrict, and divide our spirits such as religion, social and economic status, gender expectations, and more. Our spirits are meant to soar like an eagle. Essentially, I'm asking you to cast out all your preconceived ideas about life and death. Along with that, you need to eliminate doubt and skepticism, defensiveness, ego, fear, and trepidation. Those are the things that create noise and chaos in your mind and cut you off from the greater good, the spirits, the love, and the divine forces that are all around you.

Once you open your mind and heart, you will be amazed by what streams into all that space you've cleared away. What you'll find is that deep inside yourself, in your authentic core self, you already know everything I'm about to tell you to be true.

When you sit with these truths, you will finally be able to break the negative cycles you have been living with. You will be able to understand the impermanent and irrelevant titles and roles you have created or that have been cast upon you, making you feel different, not accepted, or as if you don't belong. If you listen closely to this inner wisdom, you will hear it whispering in your ear, telling you that you are exactly where you're supposed to be. Right here. Right now.

Soon enough, you will understand why you were born and why you continue to exist.

Remember when Dorothy's world turned from black and white to color? It's one of my favorite moments in *The Wizard of Oz* because it reminds me of something I see every day in my teachings. People who thought their lives were one way, without color and texture, suddenly feel their eyes have been opened and they can see all the beautiful, glorious colors of the world. I truly hope that this book will turn on the great shining light of The Universe so that you can see all the rich, vibrant colors that were always around you, just hidden out of sight.

Now forget about what you thought was your *sole* purpose in life and join me in discovering your true *soul* purpose. This book is my word, this book is the truth, this book is me, and this book is you.

With love and peace,
Kim Russo

Your Soul Purpose

Indestructible: Understanding Frequency, Vibration, and Universal Laws

> "To change, you must face the dragon
> of your appetites with another dragon:
> the life-energy of the soul."
> —RUMI

JUST AS you need to understand simple arithmetic—addition and subtraction—to move on to algebra or geometry, you need to understand a couple of basics about the spiritual world to move on in this book. I'll break it down into two sections to make it easier to follow. If you know me, or my work, you know I always say it as simply and straightforwardly as I can. Don't worry—you aren't getting a grade as you did in math class. Just read and enjoy!

THE SOUL

To find anything, you have to know what you're looking for. You couldn't find a Chapman stick in the middle of Times Square if you didn't know what a Chapman stick was. (I'll tell you eventually what it is.) So, if you're going to find your soul purpose, you have to begin by understanding exactly what a soul is.

Let me explain.

I'm a doubter. A questioner. No matter what you tell me, I'll ask the *why*, the *where*, the *how*, or the *who*. Even though I consider myself to be a spiritual person living a spiritual life, I need a little science in order to fully back up what I'm being told by the spirit world to get me on board.

I don't want to get too complicated and textbooky here, but to understand me and the world where I communicate, you need to understand quantum mechanics. Let's start with something that anyone who paid attention in seventh-grade science class knows for sure (science was my favorite subject, by the way): The total amount of energy in the universe has always, and will always, be the same—even as the universe expands. The form that energy takes is constantly changing. Or, if you prefer to listen to Einstein instead of me: *Energy cannot be created or destroyed. It can only change from one form to another.* And, again, this is seventh-grade science. Everything in the universe is made out of indestructible energy.

Quantum mechanics is the study of this energy. As scientist Niels Bohr said, "Everything we call real is made of things that cannot be regarded as real." In other words, energy is all there is, all we are. Intense magnification of atoms (the building blocks of everything that is) shows that they are made up of spinning vibrations of energy. When you focus in closer and closer on an atom you see nothing: a physical void. An atom has no physical form. It is simply radiating energy. Additionally, each atom gives off a unique energy signature. Every human on Earth, and every human who ever was, is composed of these atoms, which radiate energy in ways that are unique to each person. Whether a body is there or not, the person—those radiating atoms—still exists.

In the words of Johns Hopkins physics and astronomy professor

Richard Conn Henry, "Get over it, and accept the inarguable conclusion. The universe is immaterial." In other words, the realm where I communicate by interpreting the language of energy is within the authentic and true state of the universe. The realm where I reside as I type these words, and where you reside as you hold this book in your hands, is within the *illusion* of material or physical permanence.

Wait a minute, you're saying. Wait one gosh-darn minute!

I'm waiting.

Okay, I've waited long enough. I know what you're wondering. Since all matter is atoms and all atoms are radiating energy, and since all energy cannot be created or destroyed, does that mean . . .

Yes. It means that all the people who have passed on, who we think are no longer with us, are really just in the next room (as my spirit guides like to say).

One day, while I was meditating, hoping to understand more truths about the soul and its purpose, pictures started flooding into my mind's eye. I was shown a vision of a beautiful Victorian-looking birdcage, standing approximately five feet from the ground, made out of an antique-like sturdy metal. In this cage was a beautiful bird with vibrant colors, peacefully perched as if she didn't have a care in the world. After watching this slideshow, I immediately began to understand the analogy of the bird and its cage. Let me explain it to you here.

If your body is the cage, your soul is the bird. This beautiful, feathery bird will certainly live in that cage for a while, eating the pebbles of seed. But, really, the cage is irrelevant to the bird. The bird does not exist simply because there is a cage to hold it. In fact, a cage isn't even the ideal place for the bird—the tree is. If and when that bird leaves the cage, it doesn't cease to exist—it just ceases to exist in that cage. Really, the bird has flown into the lush, leafy tree. The tree is the ideal environment for the bird. It is the place where it is in perfect harmony with its surroundings, getting all of its needs met. Being in the tree is like being connected to The Divine. Now, you might come home from work, stand in the middle of your living room, and start hollering because your beautiful bird is gone. The cage is empty and there are some yellow feathers strewn across the floor, but no bird. At that moment, it might be difficult to believe that the bird still exists. You miss seeing it in your living room; you miss its sweet, dulcet song. But if you could open up your heart to another dimension, the dimension of the tree—the light of The Divine Intelligence—you would see that the bird is still here. But to perceive her, however, you need to rely on senses from another dimension.

I know, I know: You want to know more. You're saying, *Kim, are you telling me that my beautiful nana, who slipped on the ice in Trenton, New Jersey, broke her hip, and never recovered, is up in a tree?* Or maybe you're saying, *Where exactly is my uncle Bob, who went on that fly-fishing expedition in Montana, had the greatest week of his life, according to the postcard he managed to send, but then ended that week in a head-on collision?* Or, you might be asking, *How do we locate my aunt Mary Catherine, who passed on in her sleep at age 81 while on a missionary trip to Aspen, where she managed to both ski and attend services at the Catholic church?* Yes, there are many souls who are missing from our lives. Think of all the billions and billions of people, going back to when time was first recorded. Or, think of all the people going back to Ardi, the 4.4-million-year-old skeleton that was dug up in Ethiopia. Each person who has existed since the beginning of time, since Ardi, was made up of atoms, of an indestructible but fully mutable store of energy. A soul!

Where that soul goes after leaving the cage of the body is up to the soul. Free will extends across the dimensions. A soul—let's go back to our bird—might leave the divinity of that tree and enter another cage. In that new cage, with a new family, maybe in a new country, she'll learn the lessons she needs to learn, the lessons that will lead her to full enlightenment. Or, maybe our bird isn't ready to be rehoused yet and she's decided to stay home, near that empty cage, checking in on the cat that was left behind. (My Aunt Mary would do that because, really, who could love Philomena, her mangy, dagger-tailed, one-eyed cat, other than Aunt Mary?)

Other souls, as many of you can attest, hover near their loved ones. One might be watching over you now as you read this. And some souls are shining with their lights as bright as the sun. They're in the spiritual realm, the metaphorical tree for our metaphorical bird: their natural habitat, the place where the fit is perfect. They are souls who have demonstrated pure love and understanding while living here on Earth. They have lived many lives, paid their karmic debts, and have evolved into the great spiritual teachers of all time. I don't think I'm going out on a limb when I say that people like Mother Teresa or the Dalai Lama have filtered through their fair share of cages (bodies), and in doing so, have learned so much that they ascended to be part of the highest frequency in the universe: LOVE. This frequency exists on every dimension, and is ever-present, loving and guiding each one of us.

Some of you may be asking how I know all this. Well, part of it is in that seventh-grade science textbook you used to barricade the door to your bedroom to keep out your spying little brother, so you and your best friend could try on your mom's makeup you "borrowed" while lip-syncing to your favorite boy band. It was in Einstein's words, *Energy cannot be created or destroyed.* And part of it was told to me, or conveyed to me, after I learned to open myself up to receive messages from the energies of the spirit world.

You see, I was born with a gift that I didn't fully understand or use until after I was married and had my three boys. One aspect of my gift is this: I can interpret the language of energy. I can sense and descramble the energy into readable messages. This energy continually vibrates in and around you and me; I see it wherever I put my focus. (Remember, everything is made of atoms and atoms are microscopic puddles of vibrating energy.) Some of the vibrations I sense are spirits, or the souls who have left the birdcage. Using what I'll call intuition, I can understand the essence of these vibrations and the messages they're sending.

Let me explain what it takes to listen and learn from a disembodied spirit (one that has left their cage). The information doesn't necessarily come to me audibly. I mean, think about it, many of the souls I've made contact with speak languages I don't speak. And some of them passed on as infants before they were able to speak any language. But when I connect with these souls, we are not bound by the Earthly laws of time and space or language barriers; instead, the souls and I transcend these restrictions together. Souls vibrate (their atoms vibrate) at a higher frequency than us. In order to communicate with spirits, I, as a caged soul living in the dense three-dimensional world, governed by the **Law of Gravity,** must raise the vibrations of my electrical field, while the souls decrease theirs. We connect and communicate when we have reached the same vibrational frequency. These frequencies, or signals, can actually be measured by devices such as EMF meters, or electromagnetic field meters.

If you can imagine TV, radio, or cell-phone signals, then you can imagine the electromagnetic frequency emitted by spirits. The energy they put out needs to be filtered through a medium that can properly read the signals and then deliver the message for useful purposes. Television sets are the medium for cable signals. The radio is the medium of AM, FM, and Sirius signals. And I am the medium for soul signals. It's really easy to understand when you look at it like this—right?

Usually, when I talk to a disembodied soul, I am presented with symbols that I see in my mind's eye These visions appear on the same screen in my mind as daydreams or memories. The symbols are visual references that my brain and body feel and understand in the same way as when you imagine a picture of a juicy burger (veggie or meat) with a side of salty fries. It doesn't matter what language you speak, or what time period you live in—everyone gets the meaning behind a picture of a delicious burger (and let us not forget the fries!). There are times when the images are more obscure and I feel like I'm playing a game of charades. As if I were to see a Chapman stick (which is, by the way, a musical instrument that looks like a guitar neck with a missing body) I might not quickly recognize the feelings running through me. Eventually, though, as more images came up, I would get the message.

If you want to better understand how I read spiritual images and messages, go on the internet or pick up a science journal and read about mirror neurons. These are clusters of cells in the center of your brain. These cells fire up equally when doing an act—like laughing or kissing—and when observing an act. So, if you watch someone kissing— I mean really watch them—your mirror neurons will fire off the same synapses as they would if you yourself were kissing. In other words, through your mirror neurons you know and understand, in a firsthand way, the kiss you're observing. The separation between observation and live action does not exist as far as mirror neurons are concerned. When I'm reading vibrations and seeing the images, I am like an entire body of mirror neurons. Though I am not the actual vibrations (souls) I am encountering, I feel them and understand them as though I were them. And, in this way, I understand their message no matter what language it's being sent in, or even if the message is coming from a being who passed on before it had learned a language. After all, the soul is ageless.

If you've seen my shows or met me in person, you know I'm a normal working mother and wife. I just happen to have been gifted with access to other dimensions. Talking with the world of spirit is no different from doing sign language to communicate messages to people who are hard of hearing or deaf. For over 20 years, as I've communicated in other dimensions (some days speaking more to spirits than the living), I have collected a storehouse of information about how to improve the human experience in this dimension on Earth. The larger and more important messages that are shared through me are meant to be shared with you as well. One thing I am certain of: I am a messenger of love, light, and compassion. And as I've witnessed time and time again, those receiving these messages walk away with their lives transformed.

Don't get me wrong—these messages penetrate deep into my soul, helping me, just as much as they help you. I am certain my guides intend it to be that way. I'm still here in my cage, right? Just because I am able to interpret energy and translate it as a language doesn't mean that I have mastered all my Earthly lessons. We are all a work in progress—I am writing this book because my personal spirit guides have instructed me to do so. The three-dimensional material world, planet Earth, is at a changing point and needs the influence and the love of the spirit world now more than any other time in history.

If you understand the concept of evolution, then you know that nothing stays the same. As souls, we are meant to keep growing and evolving into the highest expression of love and light. When you decided to return to the three-dimensional world—yes, you decided to come (for more on this read my previous book, *The Happy Medium*)—you were joining the great plan to raise the collective consciousness of humanity. This raised consciousness brings us all closer to love and closer to the source of the very existence of all that is.

As I discussed in *The Happy Medium: Life Lessons from the Other Side*, we are all a chip off the old block of one Divine Source of life. Divine energy is best experienced through feelings via your heart center, rather than rationalized thinking via your brain. Although I will try my best to explain the essence of The God Force throughout this book, I am sure I will fall short, as our human perception of God cannot be explained with words of any language. While we are existing inside our Earthly bodies, we are extremely limited on many levels, especially in our thinking, to comprehend the greatness and the magnitude of the essence of God. What we do know, however, is that God's love is immeasurable, unconditional, and never-ending for all his creations.

When we look all around us, especially in nature, it is apparent that there is a higher intelligence and consciousness that has orchestrated each particle of matter to vibrate at a certain frequency, allowing it to express its creation through its own physicality, in its own ecosystem. Since this higher cosmic intelligence has breathed life into every living organism, of course this includes both you and me. On the Earthly plane, human beings are the highest form of intelligence of all of God's creations. Therefore, as sparks of this divine pure energy, we express ourselves through our physical bodies. In order to remember who we truly are, we must look inside our hearts, and just as with our bank accounts, as long as we remember the code to gain entry (password hint: "LOVE")—we have continuous access, 24/7, to this abundance of love and intelligence.

TGF can be seen when we look into another person's eyes. We have all heard that the eyes are the window to the soul. Have you ever noticed that some people's eyes shine so brightly, with a brilliant sparkle that they can light up a room? Most likely, these are people who have a pretty good connection with TGF and their own soul's mission. They are happy to be alive and they live their life with meaning and purpose. Not only can this light be witnessed through a person's eyes, this cosmic energy is the vital life-force that keeps our hearts beating without us even having to think about it.

Now do you understand what your soul is? I think you do, right? If not, take heart—I will do my best to help remind you of the power that lies within you and how you can gain exclusive access to it. I use the word *remind* because this is not a new concept for your soul to learn. Your true self, or your soul, already knows these truths, but a veil of forgetfulness has been hanging over you like a dark shadow. Now it's time for the darkness to fall away as a new day is dawning. Your spirit is restless and you are gently waking up to another reality. Once we've tapped into our soul, there is nothing that can hold us back. We are everything. We are part of The Divine. And we are one: your soul and mine, united in a single energy force. With the divine knowledge of TGF, together with the help of the spiritual realm, we will evolve together and elevate all of humanity. We can break the chains of separation, moving collectively toward love, compassion, and peace instead of hate, war, and fear.

UNIVERSAL LAWS

Before we go forward, I want to speak about some of the laws that govern the universe—and, since we are part of the universe, these laws certainly apply to each and every one of us. I'm not referring to Earthly laws such as the ones that enforce wearing your seatbelt when you drive (though, I highly recommend wearing one); I'm talking about laws that were created by The God Force the moment He created the universe. They are laws that have always been intact and will always be intact in order to keep the system running in the way that TGF intended. The Universal Laws, also called spiritual laws, are like those inflatable bumpers they put in bowling lanes for kids—they keep the ball rolling in the right direction. For us, for souls, they keep you moving toward the light, toward The Higher Power, and toward The God Force, which is within all of us. Without these Universal Laws, souls would be spinning out of control, hither and yon, like a bowling ball rolling across a blacktop with nothing to stop it but the random first thing it hits. These laws create balance and work against chaos. They are as real as the universe itself and cannot be denied or ignored.

Even when your life is turned upside down and you can't see how you will get out from under, these Universal Laws are constantly in motion, working behind the scenes, to find the most perfect solution for any dilemma you may have. Recognizing these laws can only assist you in reaching toward The Divine within you. These laws will guide you as you navigate the way to know yourself, and to understand yourself and your soul as an extension of The God Force.

All spiritual laws are important, but I am only mentioning the ones that pertain to the work you'll be doing throughout this book. These laws are like a well-orchestrated symphony, perfectly synced. When we understand and apply these laws as we reach toward our soul purpose, we, too, will sync with The Universe. Imagine the beautiful music you'll make when your soul is fully aligned and tuned in to The Universe!

Before you read through these laws, mark this page with a bookmark or a sticky note (or just dog-ear it). Each of these laws will come up in later chapters. When they do, you might want to look back here and read them again.

1. **The Law of Divine Oneness.** Everything is connected to everything else. Each breath we take changes The Universe. We are inextricably connected. Remember this with each act you take and each decision you make, for it has the power to change the world.

2. **The Law of Love.** In the beginning, God showed His love by creating man and woman. He later showed His love by allowing His son-ascended, Jesus, to come to Earth to demonstrate divinity through unconditional love and compassion. That was the greatest display of love ever made. All of us are made of love and are capable of love as great as God's. When you love God with all your heart, you love yourself and each other. The **Law of Love** is the highest law of them all. Love transcends suffering and bypasses the physical laws of limitation. Our soul needs love like a plant needs water. We need to embrace love to live our most authentic life—and like an astronaut focuses on the moon as his final destination, so too must we strive and focus on the power of unconditional love as our final destination. Love saves. Love heals. Love is everyone's true heritage of infinite possibilities and eternal joy. Love is the medium for all miracles.

3. **The Law of Balance.** Each movement you take, each time you act in any way, your motions ripple through The Universe and affect everything that is. If what you do throws off the weight of The Universe, if it throws off the weight of your family, or job, or friends, or vacation—The Universe adjusts to rebalance. Another way to

think of it is this: *For every action there is a reaction,* whether you like it or not. Some people call this karma, which is the physical manifestation of the **Law of Balance** based on a person's free will choices. Most people, however, think of karma as a personal form of punishment serving as payback for something awful they did in the past. But karma isn't personal; it's simply the scales of The Universe adjusting and readjusting for every tilt and bounce until harmonious balance is achieved. One thing to keep in mind: The **Law of Balance** is continuously at work on behalf of your soul, even when you depart the physical world. Your soul is bound by this law, no matter what dimension you are vibrating in. This is good news because we have many chances to balance out our karma, or our actions.

4. **The Law of Vibration.** Everything in the universe is made of atoms. Every atom is continuously in motion and vibrates. Thoughts vibrate. Feelings vibrate. Words vibrate and emotions vibrate. Since there is nothing that can't be reduced to atoms, there is nothing that is not vibrating. As you read this book, you will learn about increasing the energy inside you, also known as your vibrations. The ultimate goal is to harmonize your vibrations with the light of The God Force. Sit back and watch the magic happen.

5. **The Law of Resistance.** Resistance is the opposite of surrender. People think that when they resist something, they are staying away from it. The opposite is true. Whatever you resist will certainly persist. Resistance is a power, an energy that pulls in the very thing you wish to repel. Think of it this way: If someone says, "Don't think of cute kittens," what do you think of? Cute kittens, of course. That's the **Law of Resistance.**

6. **The Law of Motion.** This one is hard for humans, in our three-dimensional bodies, to accept. It's the law that everything changes—no matter what. You can't stop it. Trying to stop change is simply engaging in a losing battle of resistance. When you accept that everything changes, continuously, you can flow. In fact, the only way through the **Law of Motion** is to "go with the flow."

7. **The Law of Attraction.** This law appears many times in this book. Once it's pointed out to you, you won't be able not to see it in your life every day. The **Law of Attraction** says that like attracts like. Low frequencies attract other low frequencies. Good attracts good. Evil attracts evil. It's like water—the way drops of water draw toward each other to create bigger drops. Since The Universe does not discriminate when delivering the goods, it only responds by what it hears through the messages you are constantly generating in your mind. Be careful of your thoughts, because they become things. This law implies: If you want more love in your life, you must feel love, give love, receive love, and BE love. If you want more peace in your life, you must first master being peaceful.

8. **The Law of Polarity.** This law states that everything in nature is dual, has an opposite counterpart, is part of the same continuum, and is always connected to its whole. If you remember what you've learned in science class, all things in the universe are either negatively or positively charged. This includes everything from an atom to plants to humans, etc. The male atom is positively charged and the female atom is negatively charged (not negative as in emotions, but rather negative as in nucleus). Therefore, all forms of creation are formed by joining both male and female energy. In the human body, we can find female energy inside of the male and vice versa in the female. If we use the example of a thermometer, we can see two extreme temperatures, hot and cold, and somewhere in the middle we can find warm. We see the polarity here in the two opposite temperatures of hot and cold. The warm temperature is where we can see the **Law of Balance.** So, in order for us to understand one thing, we must also understand its opposite. We can't see the light without seeing its polar opposite, the darkness. We can't know joy without knowing anguish. In understanding the **Law of Polarity,** we have to understand that nothing is as simple as its single side. The **Law of Polarity** is a fundamental law and when it is put in motion, it opens up the space to create, manifest, achieve balance, and practice gratitude. Part of being an evolved soul is the ability to see past the superficiality of one side so as to embrace the whole.

9. **The Law of Gratitude.** Gratitude is a powerful law. When put into practice it changes your vibrational frequency and changes the frequencies of those around you. To practice gratitude, you must put forth great positive energy into The Universe. It is your way of telling The Universe that you are grateful for all blessings, big and small. It is your way of saying thank you when a favor appears. Even if what you receive does not seem favorable, anything that helps you get closer to God can be considered a favor. We may not see it right away, but eventually it becomes as clear as the nose on our face. Just as with any other blessing that is bestowed upon us, material or otherwise, a simple thank-you should suffice. Through the act of practicing gratitude, we can already apply two of the great spiritual laws: the **Law of Attraction** (staying in a state of gratitude will attract more things to be grateful for) and the **Law of Polarity** (we would not be able to practice gratitude unless we had first experienced its opposite—judgment, criticism, and suffering). In acknowledging the greatness of all He created, gratitude is surely a quicker way to get closer to God and to receive unlimited blessings from The Universe.

2

Who Are You? Finding Your Worth, Letting Go of Fear, and Learning to Be Authentic

> *"Knowing yourself is the beginning of all wisdom."*
>
> —ARISTOTLE

"WHO ARE you? (if you were a teen in the '70s, you might echo with "Who, who, who, who?"). It seems like a simple question, but rarely do I encounter anyone who answers it correctly.

In the first pages of this book, I wrote of the soul, what it is, and how it resides inside our bodies. Some of you might be aware of your soul, and others might question how, if at all, it is the driving force in your life. So let's get into all of that while we look at *who* you are.

If you know my teaching style, you know that I like to break everything down to its simplest form. As we move forward, keep the thought of your soul in the back of your mind. In this chapter, we're going to figure out exactly who each of us is. In doing this, the **Law of Polarity** (page 12) comes into play. The **Law of Polarity** helps us to define things, including ourselves. So with this law in mind, let's not look at what we are. Instead, let's jump into our duality and look at *what we are not*.

Through my 20-plus years of conversations with the spirit world, this I know for sure: You are *not* a human being having a spiritual experience. Instead, *you are a spiritual being, having a human experience.*

I realize this truth is hard for most of us to see and accept. We live in a physical world, we fill our lives, our homes with physical things—furniture, rugs, drapes that we should get dry-cleaned once a year but never do. We dress ourselves in clothes from the mall or from an online catalogue. Many of us drive cars. And those cars are filled with more things from the physical world. I have a friend whose van contains enough salty, cheesy snack foods, library books, and water bottles strewn across the seats that you could live there comfortably for a week. We are covered with and practically buried beneath things. And then, every holiday, birthday, or anniversary, we buy more things. We box, wrap, and ship things. At Christmas we fill giant stockings that wouldn't fit on anyone's foot with even more things. I'm not saying you shouldn't have things! I have a house, car, all the same stuff you have. And I love Christmas and filling giant Christmas stockings that hang on my mantel. What I am saying is that if you aren't paying close attention, or you aren't looking for your soul purpose, it's pretty easy to mistake these things as your identity.

One of my favorite aunts has frequently said to me, "If you have a nice handbag with pretty shoes to match, you'll always have the attention of others!" I love this aunt and appreciate any advice she might have, but when she says this I always wonder: Is the person noticing *me*, the real me, when what has caught their eye is my fancy handbag and nice shoes?

The problem is, the things we collect don't provide our basic needs and desires. Material objects fail to feed our souls. Yes, a nice car is comfortable and it's quiet on bumpy roads. And there is something peaceful and lovely about sitting in a perfectly clean, tastefully decorated room. But neither the room nor the car feels anything toward you. You might love them, but *they don't love you back.* And within the void of love the illusion of happiness is born.

Here's another way to think about it. Pretend you are the last person on Earth, wandering around, let's say, Los Angeles, all by yourself. Every door is unlocked, every car has a key in the ignition, every closet is open, every store is open. You can have *everything*, you're like the sultan of the world! But, again, there are no other people. Let's say you walk into a cool, modular house in the Hollywood Hills, and you make yourself some organic, fermented, healthy lunch in the wide, gleaming kitchen with windows from floor to ceiling. Then you go into the living room–size closet, change 15 times, and walk out with the most stylish, expensive clothes you could find. Next, you go to the garage and pick a car. You like the white convertible with white leather seats. Then you drive that car all over the empty freeways of Los Angeles. Yeah, going fast might be fun for a few minutes. But eventually you'll realize it's just you. In some clothes. In a car.

When you're alone in the world with all those riches, do you really love that stuff? Does it really do anything for you? Remember, the stuff doesn't love you. It doesn't hear you. And even though you're wearing it and driving it, it isn't you. It's not even an apt representation of you. The pursuit of things is an endless chase that only sends you from store to store without providing you with the one thing you really need: love. We have things but, *we are not our things.*

You may be saying, *Yes Kim, I know I am not my things, but these comforts sure make my life a lot easier.* Well, newsflash! Of course they can and they do make your life easier. Heck, I even love my fair share of feel-good or luxury items. I was in New York the other day and saw a coat that I loved. It was the right cut for me (midthigh), right color (red), and right fabric (wool gabardine). Then I visualized all the coats I already own, and the coats I've barely worn. This was followed by the vision of my jam-packed closet, which I've been meaning to clean out but haven't had the time to do so. The thought of this overindulgence, combined with the thought of how many less fortunate people are in need of a warm coat, immediately stressed me out. I asked myself whether my life would be any better with one more coat. The answer was no, of course not! I knew I needed to be more disciplined by not giving in to my impulses. This immediately prompted me to remember the **Law of Balance** (pages 10–11). Everything is connected, everything is relative. As long as you maintain balance, things will not be the end of you.

By the way, the thought of buying that new pretty coat sparked another important thought that forced me to clean out my closet sooner than I would have. And I donated some of my lightly used coats to people in need. I felt so much lighter in more ways than one. If you're working too hard to buy luxury items, remember the saying: *All work and no play makes Jane a dull girl.* Another way of saying that balance is key.

Most Americans are materialistic to some degree. But my friend Steve isn't like that. Steve grew up in TV show–worthy opulence. He was the youngest of 10 kids in a Catholic family of great prominence. A prestigious American university is named after his mother's family and an entire geographic area in a big American city is named after his father's family. Steve grew up with nannies, a live-in cook, and live-in housekeepers. He spent summers in Europe, where his parents rented entire floors in the nicest hotels. Sometime in his 20s, Steve realized the spiritual void in the world of things and flew off to California, where he lived in a commune in the mountains of Santa Cruz. Steve's job in the commune: delivering babies. In the six years he was there, he delivered 37 babies. Everyone in the commune loved Steve. He was Steve, the midwife. Steve, the doula. Steve, the baby deliverer. This is how others saw him and this is who he thought he was.

Until he woke up one day and felt like he was living the wrong life. He had this terrible feeling that who everyone thought he was wasn't really who he *was*. The only problem was, Steve didn't know who he was if he wasn't the hero of the commune. Steve, at a young age, had intuited and felt one truth: that he was not defined by what he owned. Perhaps the reason for his dilemma was because he was born having every luxury item under the sun and he didn't know what it was like to want or need anything, but he hadn't yet discovered another equally important truth: that he was not equal to the work he did on the commune. We have jobs, but, *we are not our jobs.*

I know a woman who now lives in Boston—let's call her Elise. She's as smart as anyone I've ever met, and academic, too, with degrees from many universities. As a child, Elise was terribly insecure about how she looked. With her dark hair and even darker skin, Elise didn't match anyone on television. This was when all people on TV seemed to be the offspring of the Brady family, blond and blue-eyed. What Elise erroneously deduced from the images of people in the media was that she was terribly ugly. When Elise went off to college, her striking looks suddenly garnered attention. This was startling to her—flattering, of course, and electrifying. The attention gave her a certain high that she'd never felt before.

It wasn't long before Elise wasn't happy with being "uniquely beautiful Elise." She wanted more, bigger, better. First, she went to a surgeon and had her breasts enlarged. Later, she got liposuction. By the time she was in her forties, she'd had eight different surgeries. Still, with all these tweaks, lifts, and expansions, Elise never felt pretty enough. As she aged, panic set in. Each new line on her face, or pound gained, made Elise feel like she was careening toward disaster.

Most of us suffer a lesser version of what Elise has suffered. We try to control our bodies—reroute them from their natural course—with the hope that a TV or magazine body will make us worthy of the time and adoration of others. It never has worked, and it never will work. You might get a few glances and, if you're working in certain fields, you might even make money off your body. But no matter what you get back for how your body *looks*, you will never feel that *you* are being seen, heard, or valued. Deep inside each of us is the intuitive knowledge that we are separate from our bodies. When attention and praise are lavished on a body that is in fact separate from *you*, an unsettling feeling will seep through your veins. That feeling is the disconnect between who you are and your body. We have a body (temporarily of course) but, *we are not our bodies.*

I have a client, let's call her Chloe, who spent her twenties and thirties trying to create a perfect world for her husband and children. Chloe's mother had suffered from depression and took to her bed for days at a time, and when she did emerge she was usually furious about something not worthy of fury—the dishwasher not emptied, or the trash bin being full. In those furies Chloe's mother threw dishes against the wall, breaking plates the way they sometimes do at Greek weddings. Chloe's dad, when he was home, was distant and remote, as if he wanted to make sure that Chloe and her mother knew that home was the last place he wanted to be.

Chloe vowed she'd never have a home like that. And she didn't. Her house was spotless, gourmet dinner was on the table every night, and she even packed gourmet lunches for her kids—meals that would require chopsticks or a linen napkin.

Yes, Chloe should be commended for how she cared for her family. Lucky them, right? But at night, when the dishwasher was running, the kids were in bed, and her husband was conked out in a chair with the *Wall Street Journal* draped over his face, Chloe felt utterly lost. As if she didn't have a purpose if she wasn't serving her family. *Who am I?* she asked me.

And then there's Lucinda. Lucinda moved to the United States from Colombia with her mother, Doris. Within a couple of years of settling here, Doris developed early-onset Alzheimer's. Search the globe, and I promise you will never find a better caretaker than Lucinda. Lucinda rarely complained. She was happy her mother was alive, though she always admitted that the docile, simple woman she was caring for bore little resemblance to the feisty fireplug of a woman who used to jog down busy Queens sidewalks to get exercise on her way to the grocery store. Friends and neighbors speculated that Lucinda would be relieved when Doris finally passed on. She'd be liberated and maybe she'd go out on a date, or even just go to a movie one night.

So what happened when her mother passed on? Lucinda was completely lost. Crying on the phone, she told me she didn't miss changing adult diapers, or washing the linens for the fourth time in a week, or getting up in the middle of the night when the bewitching hour hit and her mother wandered the apartment looking for cats that didn't exist. It wasn't so much that she missed her mother—as I said, that person had checked out years ago. She cried because she felt utterly lost. "Who am I," she asked, "when I'm not taking care of Mami?"

Though her efforts with her mother were charitable, generous, and remarkable, Lucinda still was not her mother's keeper. Just as Chloe was not her children's and husband's keeper. Remember, *we are not our roles.*

There are many different paths and turns that lead us to the roles we have. We were cast into some of them as kids: the smart one, the fat one, the funny one, the hard one, the easy one. Some we created later, like Elise, who became the woman with the hot body. Many roles were handed to us by bad or good fortune, like Lucinda, who became the caretaker after her mother's illness set in. And many we chose, because we thought we were recreating ourselves into something better than our parents, such as Chloe, who became the perfect wife and mother.

Problems occur because most of us outlive our roles. Children grow up and move out, marriages end, jobs change, people retire and pass on. Suddenly we're unable to play our roles, but we don't know how to part with them. These roles have become our identity: the story of ourselves that we have been broadcasting, or want to continue broadcasting, to the world. But hanging on to these roles hinders our growth and ability to move forward. It hinders our happiness. Even when we can see that, even when we understand that we're stuck and miserable, we often don't let go of our roles.

I frequently get calls from people who ask me to come in and clear unwanted spirits in their home. The funny thing is, usually when I get to a house, ready to do my ghost-busting ritual, the owner suddenly realizes they're attached to these poor souls who have opted to hang out with them instead of gravitating toward the light. They mention that the soul's been there through the dog getting sick on baking chocolate, the kids having chicken pox, or the terrible dinner that started a small kitchen fire. An hour before I get there, they hate the disruption. Once I'm in their living room, they feel attached to it. You see, humans are innately resistant to change. We become comfortable in what we know—even if what we know is disruptive or harmful. It is in times of discomfort that we can benefit by understanding the **Law of Resistance.** This is the law that enforces the persistence of whatever you resist. In other words, by fighting against natural forces, you engage those very same forces and give them power with your thoughts, keeping them alive and attracting them right into your energy field. When we surrender to those forces, they lose their power, and we are free of them. We might say we don't want something, but there also might be the comfort of familiarity in the discomfort, so we engage the **Law of Resistance** to keep alive the thing we know well, even if it's not good for us. This is true of bad relationships, harmful roles we might take on, or habits that are detrimental to our health and well-being. It's also true of the story we use to define ourselves.

When we first meet someone new, we are usually eager to find out our new friend's *story.* Just about everyone likes other people's stories—especially the bad stories! Perhaps we are drawn to the bad stories so as to compare them with our own, and very often we realize that our stories may not be as bad as we once thought. Think of all the reality shows where we can't help but get caught up in the wacky *stories* of the characters, keeping us glued to our TV sets as we watch new complications unfold, week after week. Even the news and newspapers are on an endless search for a good *story*.

For the purpose of this book, each of us must look at our own story, the one we have created around ourselves and our lives. It is very common for us to take comfort in our familiar story, or the belief that we *are* our story. But attachment to our story, identifying ourselves as our story, does not allow us to grow and move forward. Additionally, the story you tell of yourself is likely not even the real story of you, but instead, it's the story of the role you have chosen or the role that has been thrust on you.

The good news is that this story, this role, can change. But only if you're willing to let go of it and accept the natural laws of The Universe. Only if you look at the **Law of Resistance** and choose to surrender instead of resist.

Another spiritual law that I mentioned in the last chapter is the **Law of Motion**, the law that *nothing stays the same.* A vision that comes to my mind when I think of the **Law of Motion** is swimming in the vast blue ocean. Let's say you're out there, bobbing in the water, facing the flat expanse of sea. When a giant wave rolls toward you, you know that nothing you do can stop that wave. In fact, nothing in the world can stop that wave. You can hold your breath and duck under it, if you think quickly enough. But that's not stopping it, that's just avoiding it. And, sure enough, another wave is going to be rolling at you again within seconds. You can dive over the wave if you're good at that sort of thing. But again, you haven't stopped it and there are still more waves right behind this one. You can always try to fight it, resist it, but you'll probably end up with your face scraped on the ocean floor and a sand pie in your bathing suit bottoms. The best thing to do, the wise thing to do, is to lean into the wave and ride the crest as it pushes you toward the shore. Bodysurf!

When we resist the force of energy—when we resist spiritual and physical truths, like aging, love, and a Higher Intelligence—when we use denial, lying, cheating, or avoidance to block the waves rolling toward us, we find ourselves in more tumultuous water than what we stepped into originally.

It is when change comes in spite of our best efforts to block it—when Lucinda's mother died, when Elise thought she needed yet another surgery—that we shout out for help. In refusing to surrender to change, in trying to control the uncontrollable, we are not living in "the flow." Or, I'll say it again, acknowledging the **Law of Resistance**.

There are a couple of familiar sayings that help us surrender when faced with the **Law of Resistance**. One is "Go with the flow." The other is "If you don't bend, you'll break." These sayings are catchphrases for a reason. They echo a truth that we intuitively understand. Deep inside ourselves we know that we need to flow with the energy rather than fight against it. We have to put our hands up, dive in, and bodysurf that wave to where it takes us.

Now, let's get back to my original question: Who are you? Take out a notebook and pen—or go ahead and write in the margins of this book—and answer the questions in the quiz below. These are simple questions, though you may never have been asked any of them before. Give your gut answer, the first thing that comes into your mind. Answer with your heart. No one else needs to read your answers, so why fake it? Besides, the only way to find your soul purpose, the only way to figure out who you really are, is through raw, barefaced truth.

Everything will make sense as you read further on. Trust me on this!

Soul Search

WHO ARE YOU?

1. Who are you? Don't think too hard—just answer this question with the first words that come to mind.

2. In one or two words, how would you describe your role in your primary adult relationships (with your spouse,

children, or partner)? Are you the disciplinarian, the cheerleader, the breadwinner? Do you agree with this assessment of you?

3. Who are you when you're not with your children, spouse, partner, or any other family member?

4. Who are you at your job? How different is this from the person you are when you're not at work?

5. In one or two words, how would you identify your role in your family of origin? Were you the difficult one? The black sheep? The ignored one? The misunderstood one? Explain how your family came to cast you in that role and if they were wrong or right in how they saw you.

6. Who does your family of origin think you are now? If there are differences between who your family thinks you are and who you think you are, then explain.

7. Explain the relationship between your body and who you are. Could you be who you are if you had to hide your body in layers of loose-fitting clothes? Could you be who you are if you had to reveal your body in tight-fitting clothes?

8. Who are you when you wake up in the middle of the night and are alone with your thoughts? Is this person different from your public self? Is this person different from the person you are with your spouse or partner?

9. Look at a picture of yourself as a small kid. Focus in on that photo and try to remember your feelings at that time. Who were you then?

Read through your answers. Are all the versions—excluding how your family of origin may have cast you—essentially the same self? If so, bravo! You're a rare person who is living a fully authentic life, someone who wouldn't want to be anyone other than who they already are. You've worked hard rejecting others' ideas, criticisms, and typecasting. To a certain degree, you don't care what others think about you. You care what *you* think about you. It is likely that you've had positive role models in your life, or a strong spiritual support system that helped navigate a world where institutions, racism, sexism, ageism, classism, and so on continually try to define the indefinable, powerful individual that you are. You are in touch with your soul!

If your answers describe what looks like many different people, don't feel bad—this is perfectly normal, and one of the reasons I felt compelled to write this book. But do ask yourself if there is a pattern in how others see you. If so, face the dominant idea of you that others have, as if you were facing a mirror. Does what you see look right to you? Would you change the image others see if given the chance?

Now look at your description of your childhood self. Does this align with any other selves: Your middle-of-the-night self? Yourself when you're not at work? Or maybe yourself with your spouse or partner? Would it feel better or worse to feel the essence of that childhood self today?

Which of these selves do you feel is the most authentic and true self? What would happen if you existed in that honest and open way in all your relationships and experiences? Scary, right? But worth it!

Fear of living life as yourself, as who you really ARE, can partially be traced to childhood trauma. It might have been severe: an abusive parent or guardian; someone who claimed nothing you did was right; someone who used their power or position over you to diminish who you are. Or it could be something as simple as what happened to my friend Jessica when she was in fifth grade. Another student, Bill B., said to the class, "Jessica would be cute if she didn't have such a big nose." Jessica saw herself as Cyrano de Bergerac from that moment on—she never felt like she was pretty enough. When you carry a childhood trauma, shame, or embarrassment—when you were made to feel less-than because of your body, face, actions, intelligence, or skills—you grow a callus over those sore spots as if that might hide them from others.

And, as if childhood trauma isn't hard enough already, there's also the regrets that build up over time. Anyone who's ever left their house has eventually done something they regret. Part of growing up is figuring out what you don't want to do, whom you don't want to kiss, what you don't want to drink, which friends you don't want to have. But regrets, like shame, can make us feel less-than, or unworthy. Like those stains of shame, we thicken the invisible callus over our regrets. With shame and regret combined, this callus grows so thick that it eventually becomes a mask we wear in public, something to hide the accumulated scars of being alive. Hiding these scars bottles up energy that leads to secondary and tertiary problems in our lives: anxiety, depression, anger, frustration, a short temper, rage.

You see the equation here?

trauma/shame + regret = callus mask
callus mask + more callus mask = anxiety, depression, anger, fear

If you could trust that The Universe, The God Force, loves you in spite of your shame and regret, would you take off your mask?

I can tell you with certainty that wearing that mask and hiding your true self saps much more energy than simply living your life. In fact, living authentically doesn't sap energy at all. It frees you and it feeds your soul. Try the following exercise when you are calm and relaxed.

Light Meditation

Find a quiet space. I recommend doing this exercise while sitting straight up in a chair. Make sure your two feet are touching the ground. With your two palms resting on your lap, pointing upward toward the sky, close your eyes and imagine a brilliant ball of warm, white light descending from the heavens, entering through the top of your head. This is the point where all the negative thought patterns begin. Picture each negative thought, like a piece of Velcro, attaching itself to this light, drawing out any ideas that do not serve your highest good. Some examples of what you may want to eliminate are self-criticism, worries, fears, shame, regret, and anger.

Next, feel this warm, glowing light moving into your throat and into your chest cavity. See this light getting brighter and brighter as it touches your heart center. Picture this light as a special key that has the spiritual code to unlock and open up your heart, allowing it to expand in all directions. Now that your heart is wide open, you can easily invite more and more love into your life. As this light continues to pass through your body, know that its job is to transmute any negative debris and neutralize it into a brilliant, glowing light.

This light has no restrictions—it is anything you need it to be. Try to use it as an energy magnet, able to suck up anything that is not pleasing to your body and doesn't belong there—including any negative emotions or thoughts, toxins that cause illnesses, and anything else that blocks you from the light of your soul.

Feel this light going down your spine and spilling into your belly. Allow this brilliant light to sit there for a moment, clearing out any stored emotions from your past that have weighed you down. You are finally ready to release this energy through your solar plexus—notice how light you feel. Since the purpose of this light is to serve you, allow its power to pass down each leg and journey through the bottom of your feet, pushing out any unwanted hitchhikers deep down into the Earth.

You are now filled with crisp, clean, pure light. Sit still with this light and wait to feel the pulsating power inside you that has been there since the beginning of time. This light, this power, is your authentic self that was buried beneath years of shame and regret. Your soul and your self are one and the same.

If you can't locate this light or feel it yet, don't worry. It will come to you as we work together to find your soul purpose.

SOUL KIT

The first tool in your Soul Kit is the Blower. The Blower is a mental exercise that involves deep breathing and helps you release any unwanted energy weighing you down and keeping you stuck. Picture two openings on the top of your skull, like a whale's blowhole. Breathe in deeply and then breathe out, imagining everything that is blocking you or holding you back being pushed out that blowhole. Release all of the following through your deep inhalations and exhalations:

- Shame, regret, guilt, anger, and fear you've been carrying over the years.
- Labels and identities that others have placed on you.
- The illusion of control over your image.

BONUS TOOL: CHARITY

Volunteer, donate, or help someone less fortunate. **Give away an item that you thought defined you,** perhaps a warm designer sweater, to a person in a senior living facility. Try to part with a pair of rain boots that someone in a homeless shelter could use. Or give away a coat that has been the envy of all your friends. Observe how you feel once you've given your time and favorite items to those in need.

3

How Did I Get Here? Rediscover Childlike Intuition, Become Your Own Authority, and Return to Your True Self

> *"Every beauty which is seen here by persons of perception resembles more than anything else that celestial source from which we all are come."*
> —MICHELANGELO

OKAY, I'M sure you know how you got here biologically. At least, I hope you do! But how did you get *here?* To this place in your life? In this chapter we're going to explore the people, ways, and beliefs that led you to the exact spot you are in now—physically, emotionally, career-wise, and relationship-wise. By the end of this chapter, you'll understand *why* you are where you are.

Things might even be pretty good right now; not everyone who searches for their soul purpose is in the middle of a crisis. But even when life is going well—you are happy with your job, the kids are healthy and happy, your spouse or partner is content—there can be a nagging question of why you ended up where you ended up.

Every day when you're out in the world you can look around and see infinite lives with infinite possibilities. Could you have lived in *that* house, or been married to *that* person, or have had *that* career instead of what you have now? When you travel, many of you wonder what it would be like to live in the place you're visiting, or to live like the people you're visiting. My friend David loves Italy, which is where my father grew up. Every time he goes to Napoli, he imagines himself owning a little café where he serves the best pizza in the world. He visits Italy every year, and every year when he's on that plane flying back to Baltimore, he convinces himself that he's living the wrong life.

The fact remains, David doesn't own that café in Italy. And you're not that woman you saw accept an Academy Award last March. And there's only one man who won the gold medal for downhill skiing at the last Winter Olympics, and he isn't you. (Unless he's reading this book, in which case: Welcome!)

You're you. And you're here. In a particular place, with particular people, working or not working at a particular job. And no matter how fine it all might be right now, one can't help but pause every now and then to ask the question How did I get here? Is this what I was meant to do? Is this the person I was supposed to marry or partner with? Is this how I was supposed to carry on as an adult? Is this who I am? Is this my life?

The lives and things we want vary from person to person. David wants pizza in Napoli. Stella, his wife, wants a penthouse apartment in New York. My friend Elizabeth wants to live in a yurt in the Adirondacks. And my neighbor Buddy wants to live on a paddleboat along the Mississippi River.

The common denominator in these fantasy lives is the desire to belong. When pressed to take the fantasy farther, each of the people above will create a community for their wish. David sees himself speaking Italian and kibitzing with the other pizza makers in town. Stella sees herself gathering with her kids and close friends in the dining room for an hours-long dinner (prepared by someone else) that includes singing around the piano and, later, dancing to disco music. Elizabeth wants to live in a circle of yurts occupied only by women. And Buddy wants a hound dog and a "good sturdy woman" who loves his cooking on the paddleboat with him.

This urge to connect, to be attached to other people, is as rudimentary as the urge to breathe. Granted, some of us want to connect to fewer people (Buddy) and some of us want to connect to an entire town (David). Still, at its core, we yearn for the same thing—it's built into who we are. Infants who aren't held suffer from what's called *failure to thrive*. The damage from not being held can range from an inability to bond with other people or feel safe in the world to diseases that lead to death.

The urge to connect, which is an essential part of existence, is often ignored as we grow older and lose track of our spiritual needs. For children, taking care of the need to belong usually comes naturally. Look at any neighborhood or park, and you'll see a flock of kids hanging around together. In difficult neighborhoods where many people are dealing with highly stressful circumstances such as addiction and poverty, you still find children happily playing together in a pack. Even in neighborhoods like mine, you could drive around all day and never see another adult—you'll be sure to see kids. In most American households, adults pull their cars into the garage, click the clicker that lowers and shuts that garage door behind them, and then enter their house, virtually unseen, through the kitchen door. Kids, on the other hand, show up outside. Even if they can't find someone on the sidewalk to hang out with, they'll nudge a parent into scheduling the modern method of connecting: the playdate.

You see, unlike adults, kids haven't obscured their souls with all the things that shroud us: fear, guilt, shame, anger. For them, it's a clear shot from their souls out into the world. They intuitively understand what life is, and how they came here. It wasn't too long ago that they existed in the glowing bliss of the other side—where there are no roles, titles, or positions of status.

People often ask me if I get starstruck while filming with celebrities on *The Haunting Of . . .* or in my private consultations with celebrities. The answer is always *no*. Through my communications with the spirit world, I know for certain, that no one, anywhere, is better or better off than anyone else. The God Force shows no favoritism and gives no special treatment, as all souls are equal in the eyes of God. Human beings created ranking systems and levels of status, not God. I can hear you saying, *So you're telling me that Oprah, with her many mansions and billions of dollars, isn't better off than I am in my studio apartment in Chicago?* Yes, I am telling you that, and you can trust that it's true. Oprah is the same as you and I. The spirit inside her, which is connected to a spark from one Divine Mind, is exactly the same as the spirit inside me and you. And that, my friends, is all that matters. Oprah's house in Santa Barbara has no value in the spiritual world, nor does any other material item have a purpose there—it is only temporary and will not exist forever. The infinite soul, which is you, will exist forever and ever.

Just think of any two-year-old you know and you'll see how true this is. If you gave them an expensive watch in a nice box, which would they love more: the box or the watch? (It's probably a toss-up, though in the end, the box might win out.) Now put two people in front of that two-year-old and see which one they are happier to see: the star who just won an Academy Award or someone in their family. Yeah, the family member will always win out. Two-year-olds understand the real value of things; they don't have to search for the spiritual connection they have with the people they're close to. This is because children are innocent and pure when they arrive back to the Earthly plane; plus they remember so much of what we adults have forgotten. (Please refer to my first book *The Happy Medium: Life Lessons from the Other Side* for more on reincarnation or past lives. Also, see more on this subject in chapter 4 of this book.) Without titles, money, fame, or fortune, children go directly to what they are drawn to, which is ultimately what counts most: the spiritual center of each being. And they connect to each other on an equal playing field, unaware of the layers of falseness that get heaped onto the field over time.

As we grow, as time goes on, we are not encouraged or nurtured to be who we were born to be. Instead, our parents—most of whom have the best intentions—work at cultivating our behaviors in the same ways that their own behaviors were cultivated. They ignore the emotional center and look at exterior roles and actions. What we end up with after this process is grown (sometimes only physically), working, aspiring, *wanting wanting wanting* humans. As the work, aspiration, ambition, and desires pile up, they obscure access to the soul, like a heap of dirty laundry over a floor vent. You can't feel the air, the warmth, the energy from that vent with so much stuff piled on.

Let's look at my childhood in Queens, New York.

My father was an immigrant, and we lived in a neighborhood of immigrants, mostly from Italy, Poland, and Ireland. No one was rich. And maybe some people were poor, even though all the families seemed the same to me. It was a neighborhood of middle-class houses, narrow and two-story. Most of them were built the same year and were almost exactly alike, lined up in perfect rows like kernels on an ear of corn.

My cousins lived in the house next door. We hung out and made our own fun, but we still had our separate groups of friends. Every now and then we would all meet up and hang out on the stoops—the steps leading up to the front porches of each house. We ran from stoop to stoop, playing handball, making hopscotch courts with chalk, jumping rope, and singing *Miss Lucy had a steamboat* or winding string around our hands to play cat's cradle. When it wasn't snowing or raining we rode bikes down the sidewalk or roller-skated on skates like planks that you strapped onto the bottom of your shoes. The skates adjusted to the size of your foot, so one pair of skates could stay with you as you grew. I'll never forget the thick copper keys that came with those skates. I wore mine on a string around my neck, thinking I was so cool.

My fondest memories were of the days spent with my siblings and cousins in our backyard, swimming in our pool, singing and dancing. My dear cousin Mary was our social director. She was the oldest female cousin, and loved to recreate and direct the musical plays we had acted in, summer after summer, at a family resort located high up in the hills of the Pocono mountains; one that is eerily similar to the resort in the popular movie *Dirty Dancing*. Mary cast each of us in a very specific role, and never could be convinced to change her mind on those roles. At the early rehearsals, reminiscent of our Activities Directors, Jimmy Festa and Miss Barbara, who worked at our vacation resort, Mary would reenact each dance move, making sure it synced with its corresponding song lyric. She would often have us run through the performances over and over as if we were about to appear on a Broadway stage. She was in charge of everything, even suggesting what costumes we should wear and making sure we had matching outfits. The big show was performed in my backyard as a treat for our parents after we finished eating dinner. They loved it, and so did we. We imagined ourselves to be just like the Brady Bunch or the Partridge Family. To this day, I still remember the words to those songs, and all the dance moves.

When we weren't acting in plays, skating, playing *hide-and-seek*, or hanging out on stoops, we were brainstorming. In other words, when we weren't fully physically engaged in an act, we were mentally engaged. Using our right brains, where creative energy originates, we made up new games and negotiated the rules we wanted. Each of us had a clear vision of how things should operate, and we learned and practiced bargaining power as we hammered it all out. Not only were we using our creative sides, we were learning about finances. Like many kids in the United States, we made a lemonade stand using a card table that we set up at the end of our block across the street from the subway station. Using a pretty tablecloth with pictures of lemons on it, given to my mom from my aunt who lived in Italy, and our cardboard signs with lemons drawn and colored by us, we made what we thought was a killing. Most of our customers were our neighbors, or the fathers of our friends. I don't know if they were really thirsty after a hard day of work, or just helping us out, but we didn't care. We made our money just the same and they got a nice, cool cup of lemonade after coming off a hot, crowded subway car.

Our parents had many mouths to feed and just about everyone came from single-income families, so we weren't getting money from them. Our lemonade earnings were all the money we had, so we made what we thought was good use of it when we spent it on Mr. Softee ice cream. With the first sign of spring that filled the air, the Mr. Softee truck would drive down our street every day at 3 and 6 p.m. I'll never forget the jingle that came blaring from his truck; I could have set my clocks to his tinny music. We kids stopped what we were doing and ran down the block chasing after him, waving sweaty dollar bills in our hands, screaming, "Wait! Wait!"

When school was out and summer was in full force, we gobbled up breakfast and then ran out the door, shouting behind us, "Ma, I'll see you later!" Often, we didn't return until dinnertime. There were no tracking devices, no cell phones or iPads. We knew the rules: Don't run into the street, watch out for your sister or brother, don't spit or curse, play nice, and be home by dinnertime. Or be at someone's table by dinnertime. Some nights kids just went into the house of whoever's stoop they were playing on and ate with that family. Children were welcome at most tables, though a parent might say, "Did your mom say it was okay if you ate here?" All it took was a quick phone call home, or if my brother was on his way home, I would just tell him to tell Mommy I'm staying at Norma's for dinner.

There was a sense that we kids belonged to everyone. If you misbehaved in the proximity of any adult, any person of authority, you might get reprimanded. Rarely did anyone call your parents to report the infraction. The fact that they gave you the stern look was good enough.

In this environment, with the adults keeping tabs on the kids and acting as a giant web hanging over all the children who rolled together like a bouncing ball, life was simple and I felt safe and secure. As if I belonged somewhere. These were my people, and I never doubted my inclusion with them. I was like all children in this way: born innocent and pure, with a natural inclination to bond with others (for me, the neighborhood gang), to create (the games we invented or our lemonade business), and to express my inner joy (playing, singing, roller-skating with that key around my neck). No matter where you grew up, or what language you spoke, you as a child were naturally driven toward bonding with people, creating from your heart and soul, and expressing joy.

"So what went wrong?" you ask. "How did I get here?!"

Interestingly, that very space in which we all were so safe and connected also fed us the world of adults (some sooner than others), and adult fears and adult thoughts and adult *authority*. And these adult authorities, whose own souls were covered with a pile of emotional dirty laundry, gave us the wrong instructions for how to move forward. Or maybe they handed us the wrong tools. Instead of getting Windex, to wash away everything so our souls could shine through, they gave us mud. Misinformation. Faulty beliefs that had been handed down to them by their parents (who got them from their parents, and so on, all the way back to Adam. Or Ardi, the 4.4-million-year-old human remains found in Africa).

So who are these so-called authorities? Let's examine them and their beliefs a little further. For the most part, these authorities are upstanding people who thought they were doing a good job. (We can all list numerous heartbreaking and terrifying abuses of power, but that's for another book.) These authorities were our parents, teachers, rabbis, priests, nuns, grandparents, coaches, police, the military, and even the government, TV commercials, magazines, and newspapers. They taught us about limitations and restrictions by telling us money doesn't grow on trees. They told us to work hard, be smarter, get a good education, take a safe job with benefits, marry a sensible person who also has a good job, marry within the same religion, invest wisely, and when you get old, take this for arthritis, this if your legs twitch in the night, this if your eyes are dry, this if your eyes are too wet, this to maintain an erection, and this to come out of your depression brought on by the fact that we think there's something wrong with us because we no longer care to maintain an erection.

They also told us to be taller, blonder, to lose weight, straighten our teeth, straighten our hair, straighten our backs, wear the right clothes, polish our toes, polish our shoes. To take it one step further, we may even have heard that we need to work harder than the girl down the street who was on the honor roll, and that we should be smarter than that high school dropout hanging out on the corner smoking cigarettes, to go to a college where we'll make connections or meet a smart spouse, lose 20 pounds so that a possible spouse will be interested in us, find a job that offers a pension for when we are old and unemployed, invest in something that will carry us through old age because the chances of finding a job that will support us through old age are slim, and the chances of finding a valuable mate when being overweight are even slimmer—and why can't we be as kind and generous as our brother?!

Now let's take it even further than that—all the way to the messages we understood deep inside us: We'll never be smart enough, we'll never be pretty enough, we'll never be handsome enough, sexy enough, thin enough, we'll never be educated enough, or desirable enough, we'll never be rich enough, or have enough things like clothes, jewelry, cars, real estate, boats, or shoes. (I must admit, no matter how spiritually evolved I become, I still will always want more shoes!)

Finally, let's reduce these messages from the authority figures to their ultimate meaning: We are unworthy. We are failures. And the one message that still holds most people hostage to their false authorities, or in a perpetual state of fear and submission, is that there is not enough of everything to go around. Especially money. We were never taught about the abundances of The Universe, or that it has an endless supply of everything we need to flourish.

All these messages restrict us from our true potential—they condition us to believe that we should know our place in the world. Do you remember that to become an airline stewardess years ago you had to be over a certain height and under a certain weight? The airlines claimed this was in order to reach the luggage bins and to walk easily down the aisles. I wanted to be a stewardess, but as soon as I read the requirements my dreams were obliterated. The airline authorities told me that I was not born with the proper requirements, so I had to find a new career. Thank God I did, or else I wouldn't be writing this book!

Let's talk about social media for a minute. Much good can come out of it for those who are lonely or isolated. And who doesn't like watching a kitten video or feeling the support of your community during times of tragedy and times of joy? But there is also an unfortunate side to social media: It can help perpetuate the misinformation given to us by the so-called authorities. There have likely been many times when you've felt awful about yourself after perusing Facebook or Instagram. Just comparing the number of likes on posts to our friends' can be enough to make us feel inadequate.

I was having lunch a couple of months ago in Los Angeles with a highly successful TV producer. As a human, this woman has it all: an enviable career, riches, celebrity pals, beauty, and one of the cutest damn dogs I've ever seen. Sometime during lunch she pulled up a current Instagram post of her friend from high school. "Can you believe this?" she asked me. "Look at that picture! It's in a bathing suit. Taken from *behind!* She's the only person at our age I know who doesn't have cellulite on the backs of her thighs! Why does she get to look so perfect?!" I couldn't help but wonder what the woman with enviable thighs might be saying about the TV producer's Instagram photos. "Look at her hanging out with A-list celebrities! Look at her swimming pool! Why does she get to have a career like that?!"

In its worst iteration, social media can create an inescapable shopping cart of careers, travels, spouses, bodies, and lives we don't have. It perpetuates the lies we were told as kids. It reinforces the false directives of those false authorities of childhood. It reminds us, once again, of the ultimate lessons we learned as kids: You are unworthy, you are a failure.

What all these messages from false authorities and from social media do is to derail you from the directives that come from your soul, which you intuitively understood as a kid. Those messages were: Connect to the people around you. Live in the present. Play. Create art without fear of judgment or censorship. Enjoy your body for what it does—roller-skating, running—rather than for how it looks. Love freely and openly, without shame. (How many of you unabashedly loved a stuffed animal, a blanket, or a doll? Think how humiliated you would be now to openly love that toy.)

Please keep in mind, however, this concept, which has proved itself over and over to be true: Whenever you have achieved success, most likely you have taken control and are the authority in that area of your life. If you examine how you have achieved success, you can just apply the same rules in other areas where you seem to be struggling. What you will probably realize is that you have achieved this success likely because you believed more in yourself and your abilities than what the authority figures said that could have resulted in negative outcomes. Believing in yourself, along with determination and passion, will most certainly always render positive results.

That being said, the questions I've been asking myself lately are *Who made these people the boss of us anyway? Why should we believe them when they tell us what to do?* Listen, I'm a mother of three boys, so I know what you're thinking when it comes to boundaries and putting a lid on bad behavior. But I'm not really talking about that stuff; I'm not saying that you should stop parenting your kids. What I'm saying is that the authorities aren't really authorities. And the messages we've all been getting from these authorities are blocked from the soul and from the needs of the soul, because of how our authorities were raised.

The truth is, there is only one authority. And that authority is The God Force. Call it whatever you want, as long as you trust that it's there and understand that you are not separate from it. When you listen to the people in your life who you *assumed* were the authorities, who you *assumed* knew better, and who you *assumed* were telling the truth, you are led away from your center—from your soul. The God Force has given you all the advice you need and all the ways to enact that advice. Just listen closely and follow the instincts you had as a child—connect, play, create, and love. When you are able to listen to TGF, when you can accept TGF as the only authority, you will be able to live your soul purpose.

Take the quiz on the following page. Again, be totally honest and open. Lying diverts you from your soul and your soul purpose! Once you've assessed the ways in which you've been living out false truths handed down to you by the so-called authorities, we'll figure out how to undo that. Yes, you get a do-over in life and it starts now, here, in this very moment!

Soul Search Part I

HOW DID I GET HERE?

1. Who was the strongest authority in your family of origin? Mother, father, grandparent, foster parent, stepparent?

2. Were they unconditional, or did they rule by threats and fear? (If you don't do ___, then you can't have ___!)

3. List as many directives given to you by this authority figure as you can remember.

4. Were you or your family a part of an organized religion? List the rules to live by that you learned from that organized religion.

5. What groups, besides religious, did you and your family associate with? Girl Scouts? Neighborhood block parties? Organic gardening club? List the rules that were handed down to you from the authorities in those groups.

6. Was your family part of any ethnic or cultural group? List the rules you learned from this ethnic or cultural group.

7. Whose word did you believe at school? Teachers? Most popular kids? Principals? Coaches? List the life rules you followed that you learned from any school figures.

8. What messages from the media do you feel you believed or internalized? This can be from movies, TV

shows, magazines, print ads, the internet, billboards, and even product packaging and product placement on the store shelves.

Before we go on to the second part of the quiz, read through these answers very carefully. Take out a separate sheet of paper and organize your answers into four categories:

1. Made/makes me feel bad about my actions and deeds.

2. Made/makes me feel bad about my body, face, intelligence, or skills.

3. Made/makes me feel good about myself.

4. I believe it and still live it today.

Note there might be many rules that fit into two categories: They made you feel bad and you are currently living them, or they made you feel good and you are currently living them.

Once the rules are organized into categories, highlight or underline the ones that most dominate your thinking, or dictate how you live your life today.

To make matters easier, Part II of the quiz only pertains to those highlighted answers.

Soul Search Part II

FINDING THE COURAGE TO FACE THE TRUTH

1. Did the rules from any of these so-called authorities lead you on the path to the job or career you're in now?

2.   Is this the job or career you want?

3.   Did any of the rules lead you to your current relationship or sexual orientation?

4.   Is this the relationship or orientation you want?

5.   Do you live in a geographic area, socialize with certain groups, or belong to certain organizations because of the rules from your authorities?

6.   Is this where you really want to live? Are these the groups with which you want to spend your time?

7.   Have you ever bought products, clothes, medicines because you felt that you were not the best you could be without them?

Now look at the answers above and number them 1, 2, 3. Put a 1 by anything that is exactly as you want it: your job, your spouse, your church membership. Put a 2 by anything that is neutral in your life—you could take it or leave it. Put a 3 by anything that is not in line with who you really want to be, or who you feel you are, deep inside. Part III of the quiz pertains to everything you numbered with a 3 and maybe some of the stuff you numbered with a 2.

Soul Search Part III

1.   List the ways in which your internal self, your true self, is at odds with each item you've numbered with a 3.

2. List the rules you've picked up from the authorities that prevent you from discontinuing the actions that create the items numbered 3.

3. Ask yourself what would happen if you ignored their rules, ignored their so-called authority, and instead answered to a Higher Power (the driving force inside your soul that started off as a whisper but has suddenly become a roar)?

Yes. You'd be free.

True freedom, as Dr. Martin Luther King Jr. showed us, can only exist outside the binds of being defined by others. You are not the person the authorities in your life have decided you are. You are a perfect, solid, pure being who was always perfect, and remain so now. Your goal is to look past the rules, restrictions, and labels others have put on you and listen to the only authority, The God Force.

If it's hard for you to imagine how to look beyond the labels and expectations others have placed on you, look closer at Dr. Martin Luther King Jr. It's easy to see now that in 1955, when he led the Montgomery, Alabama, bus boycott, he was doing the right thing. But what if he had listened to the so-called authorities of the time? What if he had listened to the politicians, the laws they enacted, the people who followed, believed, and enforced those laws? The state of Alabama authoritatively declared that black people were inferior to white people. If Dr. King and others had lived with those rules, lived with that authority, *believed in it*, they would have been denying their soul purpose, their spiritual center, the roars inside their souls, the spiritual laws of The Divine, which are true and irrefutable.

I don't want to compare anyone's life to Dr. King's, or any white person's life to that of a black person in the South living under Jim Crow laws. But I do want you to understand and see clearly the faulty dynamic in your life that assumes people with authority are the people who know what's best for your life. They weren't, and they aren't.

There are only two true authorities, though in fact they are one and the same: you and The Universe, or The God Force. But since you are inseparable from The God Force, you are also part of it. If God is the sky, you are the stars. If God is the ocean, you are the fish. You can't exist without God. When you are with God, like a fish in the sea, you are in your perfect place, living your true self, your soul purpose. Taking a fish out of the sea is like taking a person away from God.

Think of the things that make you feel perfectly aligned within yourself. The acts that put you in what is called *the flow*, which is a perfect state of being when the critical voices in your head—yours and those of the so-called authorities—are completely silenced so that you exist in a perfect moment of spiritual oneness. These are moments when you are in touch with TGF, when you are the fish thrown back into the sea. These moments only come when you are being perfectly authentic and true to yourself, true to who you really are.

To be a false self, to pretend you feel or believe in things you don't feel or believe, takes an enormous amount of energy that closes you off from your authentic self; it shuts out The Divine and your soul purpose. Did you ever attend an interminably boring dinner party where you were seated next to someone who told unbearable stories about their family reunion—stories that involved people you've never met and never would meet? I recently was at a dinner party where I was seated next to the nicest man who had a wonderful smile. Well, he also had one of those photo wallets, where you can flip through a miniature photo album. With four grandchildren, there were a lot of pictures to flip through. I'm not saying these kids weren't cute. They were! But I didn't know them, I was never going to meet them, and, in a way, they looked like all kids—beautiful and perfect, the way The Divine made them.

I understood this man was a proud grandpa and I had no problem looking at his family pictures, but by the time he was telling me the story of one kid's school schedule, and when he had math class as opposed to when he had English class, this was the end of the line for me. I was tempted to use my "phone a friend" escape and run off to the bathroom with a pretend emergency call to make. In moments like that, when you are unable to be your true self (my true self was bored silly and not at all interested, as I pretended to be!), you are sapped of energy, purpose, life-force. You are a fish flopping on a pier. Now imagine a whole life like that. Maybe you feel like your whole life *is* like that—an endless dinner party, having to smile through meaningless conversations to be polite. That life, where you repress your true spirit, your soul, your divine internal self, does not allow you to shine like the stars in the sky. Or to swim like the fish in the sea. In fact, it represses all that, tamps it down, covers it with dirty laundry.

So, I am telling you now: Stop! Stop being your false self. Stop living a false life.

I can hear you asking me how you can change your life so that you are living in the flow. The answer is different for each person. Do you have to quit a job? Leave a relationship? Start a new job? Reapproach the relationship you're in? Should you parent differently? If you're like me, you've definitely heard words come out of your mouth when scolding your kids that sound exactly like words that came out of your mother's mouth. It's horrifying to see yourself as someone else, right? The reason it's horrifying isn't because your parents were so awful—chances are they were doing the best they knew how. It's horrifying because at that moment you realize that you are not being your authentic self. You are simply rehashing, recapitulating, unnaturally working to keep words alive and to perpetuate rules and ideas that aren't true to you but simply live inside you because they were placed there by someone else. The work it takes to go back to your original, true self is different for each person.

Okay, okay, now you're shouting at me! You're saying, *Kim! How can I pay my mortgage if I quit my job as a bank teller and spend my days working at the kick wheel in my garage making pottery? Because that is the place where I am in the flow. That is where I am a fish in the water!*

Let's go back a bit. I need to explain your foundation—I need you to know what is backing you up in this journey to your soul purpose.

Know this: The spirit of God dwells within you, and you within it. (Remember the fish in the ocean, the stars in the sky.) We are all connected to this spirit, connected to one Universal Mind—this mind is God's Consciousness. This consciousness has all the answers you are seeking, even the answer to how can you quit your job at the bank and spend your days making pottery. Just as the Earth knows to rotate each day, giving us beautiful sunrises and sunsets; just as the tide knows to swell and ebb each day, giving us glorious low tides where we dig through tidepools: So, too, do we naturally and easily know how to express ourselves through acts of creation and the experiences of our physical bodies. In other words, through anything that is driven by our soul and not by the rules and laws that have been handed to us, we know exactly what to do.

Maybe this will help you understand how to return to your true self: Picture a beautiful blue butterfly with yellow polka dots. Now picture her flying from flower to flower on a bush. She gracefully flits through the air as if she doesn't have a care in the world. She doesn't have 50 thoughts about the 150 things she needs to do today before she leaves one flower to jump to the next. Nor does she analyze the distance between the flowers, while worrying about the time it might take to get to the red flower as opposed to the yellow one around the corner. She just lifts off and goes about her business. She knows she will land safely on another flower soon enough. The butterfly's confidence in flower hopping isn't due to any faith she has that the flower will hold her up, rather it's the faith she has in her own wings to get the job done.

Now, you may be asking, *Kim, how can you compare me—a mother who's stuck in a carpool line and now has to hurry home to get dinner in the oven so it's ready by the time my older kids come home from sports—to a flying butterfly?* I'll tell you exactly how. You, me, that butterfly, we are all beautiful, divine creations of God. The only difference between us and the butterfly is that the butterfly, who survived the struggle to get out of her cocoon, carries on gracefully in her life without the interference of ego.

When you take away ego, you remove everything that leads you away from your soul purpose. Without ego in play, the butterfly doesn't worry about the firmness of the next flower, or failing to land on the right flower, or the possibility that she's not hitting up enough flowers today. The ego, which is fear-based, is all about perceptions: ideas of success and failure, fear of not living up to expectations, and humiliation. Without an ego in play, you go for the flower! You go with your gut, your soul! (Later in this book, we'll explore in greater depth, the problems presented by the ego).

It is possible for us to live with the same simplicity and purity of purpose as the butterfly alighting on one flower and then the next. You see, The Universe hands each one of us a road map showing the easiest route to navigate your Earthly life—the life you picked in order to push through the human cocoon. With free will in play, it's up to you whether or not you follow this map. Some of you may travel down a road less traveled, some will take the scenic route, others will go the long way around, and still others might detour through dark tunnels and over rocky, unpaved roads. No matter what route you pick, you will end up in the place agreed upon by you and Divine Intelligence *before you were born.*

Yes, you and God worked in tandem, along with Counsels of Light (your angels and guides), to decide when, where, and why you should inhabit a body in this three-dimensional plane, Earth, at this current time. It may be hard for you to remember this agreement you made with God because you can't see Him in the way you've been able to see your parents, teachers, and other people whom you've believed to be the authorities. But, I guarantee, if you close your eyes and put your hand on your heart, you will feel God's presence. You will feel the intense connection shared with The Divine. You will see that you are never alone.

Sometimes we just have to stop thinking, reasoning, and wondering in order to get back to our true selves. Sometimes we just have to sit and feel the truth within ourselves.

I'm sure you are still wondering how you can follow your passion and still be able to pay your bills. In determining what the next move should be—whether you should leave a job, change jobs, or make your next career move—you need to start by eliminating the voices of so-called authorities in your head. So banish your mother's voice, which points out how lucky you are to have good healthcare benefits; banish your dad's ideas about security and your must-have pension; banish your sister's words about you working the best hours; and banish your husband's expectations of you leaving work at 5 p.m., two hours before he leaves his office, so as to give you enough time to get home and make dinner.

Once you have silenced the authorities, dig deep inside yourself and *feel* what choice of career would make your heart sing. Notice I said *feel*, not think. The logical mind can trick you into believing that instead of being a bank teller, you should pick a different career that will bring in a higher salary. Thoughts like that are *not* coming from your soul and are not in alignment with your soul purpose. You have to walk away from the mindset that drives you to make decisions on the basis of other people's expectations of you, financial safety, security, or ego. Remember when I asked you to feel *what would make your heart sing? What is your passion?*

It has become second nature for us to do what is safe or secure based on what we were conditioned to do. Notice that I said second nature rather than human nature. Choices made by second nature are derived from our past conditioning, the "lessons" we learned from the people we believed to be the authorities. Human nature is the self you expressed as a child. It's who you were meant to be: innocent, creative, loving, trusting. I've already talked about the purity of the soul in childhood, but you can also look farther back, to infanthood. Watch a baby, before they can walk or speak. They are fully trusting, fully loving, fully open to the spiritual world. All their inclinations feed their soul purpose: love, bond, eat, sleep, smile, laugh, etc.

If you have a hard time listening to the voice of human nature, if you're struggling to find the answers to your questions, don't lose faith. When you don't know what move to make next, do nothing. Really. Nothing.

Soul Search

FINDING YOUR WAY TO NOTHING

Okay, maybe you're not going to find your way to *nothing*. Maybe it is *something*. Everyone knows that prayer is a way of talking to God. Usually it is a one-sided conversation held exclusively by you, asking for God's favor. But what you might not know is that meditation is a way of listening and receiving answers and solutions directly from God. Meditation is so easy you can do it right there, wherever you are. Here is an easy way to start. Read these directives, then set this book down and have a go at it:

1. Pick a specific question you'd like answered, or a general topic about which you need to learn more.

2. Got it? Now, sit in silence. Let any intrusive thoughts float away—you can see them as images. Let these images drift off like smoke.

3. Next, close your eyes and breathe slowly and deeply, in through your nose and out through your mouth. Do this seven times, with all your focus, all your mental energy, only on your breath. If it helps, say in your mind, *I'm breathing in, I'm breathing out . . .*

If you follow these three easy steps, the answers to your questions will filter into your mind. Do not second-guess what you have received. It is very natural to believe that you have an active imagination and the answers you received were conjured up from your own mind. This is where most of my students get stuck. They don't believe the answers they received are authentic and are from a higher source. Trust me—answers like these only enter when you're looking away, when you're watching your breath and putting your analytical mind to the side. Sometimes the answers will come in the form of a feeling rather than a thought. Whichever way you receive your answers, you must trust that these answers are coming directly from the higher wisdom of your soul.

Your divine plan was downloaded into your soul before you were born. It is already set up for you and it comes with an activation switch. You can now say yes to that plan, yes to the child inside you who started off on that plan but was derailed. God has given you authority to be the authority of your life. And I'm going to back that up by saying that I, Kim Russo, am in touch with the spirit world and fully know and understand that you, and God within you, have the authority to turn on the activation switch that will start your life of living and following your soul purpose. The green light has now been switched on. Ready? Set? Go!

See? That was easy! Now that you are your own authority, you understand that you are one with God; you have activated the switch that will lead you to your soul purpose. All you have to do is take further action.

Not so fast—don't quit your job just yet! Give The Universe a chance to respond to your decision to make a change. I need to remind you that another way we were falsely conditioned by the people we believed to be our authorities is in thinking that we know the best possible route to obtain our desired results. Yes, through your free will, you make decisions that allow you to be your own authority. In addition, even though you are never separate from The Divine Source, until you know how to listen to your soul, most directives you receive are driven by your ego, your false self. When we assume that we know how and when something is going to happen, we are usually setting ourselves up for failure and disappointment.

Soul Search

YOU GET WHAT YOU EXPECT

When your soul is aching for change, so much so that you can hardly breathe, instead of forcing change on your current situation, try not to be impulsive by jumping in with two feet. There are a few necessary steps to follow before you proceed (see list on the following page). The best course of action to eliminate the possibility of your ego mucking everything up is to give The Universe ample notice, just as you would give your boss sufficient notice before quitting your job. Chances are thoughts of change have been swirling around you for a while, but you may have not known how to proceed. Always ask The Universe to send changes that are in alignment with the highest good of your soul, as well as for the souls of everyone around you. By implementing the steps listed below, like a powerful magnet, you will attract the best possible energy to activate your much-needed transition:

1. Clearly and deliberately set your intentions for what you want, need, or expect. Focus on your expectations, however drop the expectations of how you believe everything should unfold or be delivered.

2. Write it down and be very specific and descriptive. This will help you home in on exactly what you want. Similar to when you place an order on the internet for a great pair of shoes you've been wanting, you must be careful to include the model number, size, color, etc. In other words, The Universe delivers exactly what you ordered. Making a list is a good way to help you brush away the debris of cluttered thinking so you can identify your needs.

3. Read what you wrote aloud. This will help you reconfirm your needs to yourself and to The Universe. But most importantly, be open to receiving everything that you have been asking for. Do not let your fears get in the way—especially your fear of change.

4. Surrender to time and to the ways of The God Force. When The Universe is getting ready to make good on a delivery, please know that most likely there are many moving parts happening behind the scenes, which first must be rearranged and realigned, some of which you may never learn about. Try to understand, just like a game of chess, each part of the equation has to be carefully manipulated until an open and clear path is made to usher in the new energy that will assist you in obtaining your desired results. Just sit back and wait patiently, as everything happens at the perfect time.

Here's one way to think about it: When we go to a drive-thru restaurant, we stop at the menu bar and decide what we want to order. As we pull around to the pick-up window, we expect that everything is in the bag just as we ordered. We don't give much thought to how the cook made the food, or wonder how many handlers are in place to assemble our order. The same applies when we are asking The Universe for something—it is like ordering from the drive-thru window. God, in all His infinite wisdom, is fully equipped to help you fulfill the exact plan of your soul contract. He will deliver the results you need, but it's up to Him how and when those results are delivered.

Here's one thing to remember: The Universe is always seeking balance—*balance* is a Divine Law (pages 10–11). Since you are part of The Universe, each of your desires needs to fit within the balance of The Universe. When you ask for something it should serve the highest purpose of your soul and of the souls of those around you. If you are given something that creates imbalance in The Universe, the rebalancing will come through you. This, my friends, is balance at play.

SOUL KIT

Self-Parenting

Now that you know that you can be your own authority, you can apply this authority to any area of your life. As I mentioned, and I can't stress it enough, if you look at the areas where you are most successful, chances are you've already assumed authority there. Now it's time to identify the places in your life where you still feel fear is holding you back from being your own boss. Visualize yourself in the middle of that place/job/world. Now, pretend you are your own parent—not the parent you had as a kid, pretend that *you* are the parent to *you* as your own child. You understand the child inside you pretty well, and you understand the adult inside you, too. And you know everything you have been through.

Now shut your eyes and ask yourself what you, the parent-you, should do to direct and help the child-you. Listen to The Divine Intelligence speak through what you think of as your intuition. Let this Divine Intelligence lead you. Be gentle with this child, speaking softly, with compassion and love. Let this child know they are safe no matter what they decide to do. There is no judgment here on either the parent-you or the child-you. Remind the child-you that the only way to fail is to not try. Remind the child-you that what you think of as failure is really just part of the process of growth and development. When a batter hits a home run, remember that he struck out many, many times before that home run.

When you are advising the child-you, stop and make sure that you're not echoing a belief system taught to you by someone you formerly believed to be an authority. You now know better. You know that you and God are the only authorities. After all, no one else on Earth can be your proxy and take the test—the test of your soul—for you.

Don't forget that words and thoughts carry a vibrational frequency and become real things. So choose both your words and thoughts carefully.

Finally, give the child-you permission to let go of the old patterns in order to make changes. The consciousness of God plays by different rules—rules that will work in favor of the child-you as long as those desires don't inflict pain or suffering. Simply put, when a soul has an intention to carry out what is pure and good for all concerned, The Universe conspires to make it happen.

The great thing about the self-parent: They are always accessible. As long as you are there, they're there too. Whenever you're in doubt or feel lost, break out the self-parent within you. Along with your connection to God, the self-parent will always turn you in the right direction. It knows the way!

4

Showing Up for Love: Understanding the Whispers of Your Soul by Letting Go of Fear

> *"Love is happy when it is able to give something.*
> *The ego is happy when it is able to take something."*
> —OSHO

IF I ask you to define the word *love*, what comes into your mind? Would it be a specific thought? Or rather a feeling? Some of you may think of your loyal pets who offer unsolicited, unconditional love, while others may think of the love you have for your favorite food, such as pizza. Now, what if I were to ask you to define the word *fear*? Would you think of a ferocious lion chasing you and hunting you down? Or would you feel the emotion of fear that easily sneaks back in when you remember a childhood memory of a shopping spree when you were accidentally separated from your mother and had to go to the store manager and have him announce that there is a lost child in aisle five? Love and fear: These are two of the most extreme emotions and driving forces of the human race. In this chapter I will help you to understand the true meaning of each emotion, its origin, and what role it plays in our lives. They may not be exactly what you think they are, but you'll understand by the time you're done reading the chapter.

In my early Catholic-school days, I heard over and over again, "God is love." Even if you didn't go to Catholic school, chances are you heard these words somewhere. John Lennon spoke them. Posters, T-shirts, and buttons state it. The saying has been around since—well, since John said it in the Bible. But just because you've heard these words doesn't mean you ever stopped to think about the real meaning in *God is love*. My goal for you is that, by the end of this book, you have internalized this fundamental truth.

Before I was school-aged, when the only people I knew were my parents, siblings, and cousins, I had two basic emotions: love and fear. I remember these emotions and the specific ways in which they came to me, though I certainly didn't articulate or discuss my awareness of these feelings at the time. My knowledge of love came from my parents. I felt it from my mom when we sat at the table together having lunch. She always made something warm and delicious: tomato soup and a grilled-cheese sandwich, or pasta with butter and cheese. When my dad walked in the door after work, I looked up at him and was flooded with love. We also had pets who gave me this same rush of good, calm happiness. There were dogs, cats, rabbits, birds—various numbers of each, depending on the year. Every dog was a different breed than the previous one, but they had one thing in common: They loved me and my brothers and sister. We were covered with doggy kisses on our faces, or on our scraped knees—always scabbed from roller-skating or bike-riding, or just running and tripping on the sidewalk. Giving love and feeling loved was as natural to me as breathing. I never had to seek it. It was who I was, who my family was, the dominating force in our family.

This love gave me a sense of security and made me feel that who I was exactly—Kim, who loved to laugh and scream and roll on the floor with the dogs as if I were a dog myself—was perfect just as I was. This bounty of love allowed me to feel total acceptance.

Of course, you can't see the light without the darkness, and vice versa. This is part of the **Law of Polarity,** the law that gives everything that exists its opposite. It is through these opposites, through the contrasting element that is paired with each thing, that we learn to understand all there is in our lives. So, for me to understand the love in my family, I also had to understand and learn about fear. Since fear, not hate, is the opposite of love. Read on and you'll get what I'm saying here.

When I was sent to bed each night, I climbed the stairs with trepidation. If it was dark outside, it took me a minute to shore up the courage to enter the room I shared with my sister, Susan. Susan crawled into bed without a second thought. But I lay there in terror, waiting for my father, who would check under the beds, in the closet, and behind the curtains to assure me that no one was in that room but my sister and me. After he tucked me in, turned off the light, and left the room, the terror inside me grew. I could hear the gentle clatter of dishes as my mother cleaned up the kitchen. She and my dad chatted quietly; I couldn't hear what they were saying, but I knew they were talking. My brothers were already in their beds, and though their rooms were close to mine and Susan's, they felt far, far away. Susan dropped off to sleep quickly, leaving me to fend for myself.

For hours, I lay in bed, straining to keep my eyes open as I fought off sleep to protect myself from the group of spirits who showed up at my bedside each night. I call them The Gang. These men and women, dressed in black, stared down at me. They never spoke, and they didn't move much. They simply watched me. There was no empathy in their eyes and no love emanating from these souls. These people were stoic, self-contained, standing apart from me, disconnected, while examining me. With their lips sealed shut, they told me nothing.

Because they were adults, and I'd been taught to respect and mind my elders, I presumed The Gang had authority over me. And so, sadly, I let these strangers be the boss of me. The other adults in my life—my parents, aunts, uncles, and grandparents—loved me just as I was. I felt hugged and held even when they didn't touch me. But The Gang, who didn't even offer a wink or a smile, made me feel that I was being judged. Since I had full love and acceptance from everyone else in my world, and since I innately knew that *love* is all there is, I wanted that from The Gang too. I expected them to display love the way my parents and dogs did; even a simple smile would have sufficed. But no—I got nothing but my own trembling legs and a wobbly feeling in my gut.

Intuitively, I knew The Gang was telling me to keep their visits secret. I heeded their presumed authority and lived alone with these people in my room, and my tremendous fear of them, for many, many years.

As I grew older, I realized that these otherworldly people should not be standing at the foot of my bed each night. I wondered why they weren't in a cemetery. Or in Heaven. Or Hell! My nightly fear of the ghosts was doubled, tripled even, when I thought through my lessons from catechism.

In school and at church, I'd learned a lot about Heaven and Hell. I was taught that they're real locations: The souls of the dead either rise to Heaven to sit at the right hand of God in eternal joy and love, or plummet to Hell, where they reside with the Devil and burn in flames with continuous suffering, teeth gnashing, in eternal damnation. Just hearing about Hell sent a shock of terror straight through my bones.

I believed what my teachers and the priests said when they insisted that good boys and girls love each other and never speak back to their parents or any other adult. And I believed the priests when they claimed that even if I *thought* I was being good, there were likely a few mess-ups each day. When it was repeated over and over again that I'd be lucky to make it into Heaven, my sense of dread and fear grew to biblical proportions. According to both school and church, the only way to hedge my bets was to take the extra step and go to confession, where I'd cleanse my soul just before taking the wafer and the "wine" in partaking of the Holy Communion. I was determined to end up in Heaven, or maybe I was just determined not to end up in Hell.

And so, before I had the insight and determination *not to* believe the priests, I used the Catholic loophole and marched into that confessional booth (which always reminded me of the phone booth where Underdog transformed from a dog to a superhero) to spill the beans. My sins ran the gamut from having kept a marble I found on the stoop, rather than looking for its rightful owner; to having stuck my tongue out at my sister during a game of hide-and-seek; to keeping my weekly allowance and not giving part of it to the church; to talking back to my mom when she wanted me to come in the house immediately to set the table for dinner. Then the priest brought these sins to God and asked

Him to have mercy on my poor, pitiful soul. One *Hail Mary* and three *Our Father*s later, I had my golden ticket, my *get-out-of-jail-free card*, and was back on the path to Heaven.

Certainly, my parents thought they were doing good by giving my siblings and me a strong Catholic education. And, admittedly, I learned many valuable lessons in that setting. But side by side with the message that God is love, was also the message that God is all-knowing, all-seeing, and *all-punishing*. God, the Catholic Church says, is vengeful. Fear started to creep in and I was as afraid of a God who might send me to the fiery pits of Hell, as I was of The Gang, who encircled my bed each night.

Yes, I was enveloped by love from my family morning through night. But fear, unfortunately, was a current that switched on like a light, each night when I encountered the stern and unloving faces of The Gang at my bed.

The older I got, the more I questioned what I had been taught. Why would God listen to my list of sins from a priest but not from me? The confessional booth seemed like a vehicle to take me one step away from God, not closer to Him. It was like playing a game of Telephone: me, to the priest, to God, to the priest, to me. I learned early on that I am a good communicator, so I preferred to call God directly! Also, would God really punish a child for just sticking out her tongue at her sister? If God is love, why would I be sent to Hell for not setting the table the moment my mother told me to set it? Even my mother didn't get *that* mad about my lagging on the stoop. She'd just say, "Okay, Kim, enough playtime, come inside and set the table!" But God? If I were to die after lingering outside, God—according to the priests—was going to toss my little body straight down to the crackling flames of Hell, with the murderers and molesters. Who in their right mind would call that love?!

I wondered if all this fearmongering was created to control the minds of the congregation—to keep everyone in order, obeying. Was this a way to get people to listen to the presumed authorities who wielded as much power as the mayors of small towns? After much thought and observation, I deduced this: I could feel and see *love* from my family. I could feel and see *fear* in the church. I could feel and knew in my heart that God is love. Therefore, God was in my home, in my family. And, for me, He was not in the Catholic Church. As soon as I'd settled this in my mind, I called bullcrap on the supposed authorities and stopped going to confession. My faith in God, however, remained fully intact. I knew I was loved by this unseen force.

Once I discovered my gift of being able to speak with spirits, long after the tight-lipped, unloving Gang had left my bedside, I began searching for more answers. There was so much I had intuited and felt—so much information that stirred inside me. But I had no confirmation that any of it was true.

I never want to waste any of my clients' time asking questions for my personal use, but once I make contact with a spirit, the conversation is fluid: I can't dictate or control it like a traditional interview. The spirits I meet often give me information that goes well beyond whatever a client has specifically asked. They start talking about The Universe, The God Force, and love. Fortunately, people who are open-minded enough to have called me in the first place are open to learning new things about both the three-dimensional world and the spirit world.

In one of my earliest readings, I was sitting in a tidy, suburban Long Island living room speaking to the spirit of a husband and father, Jim, who was recently deceased. I mentally asked Jim, with his widowed wife and two grown daughters present, if he had seen God yet. Jim said, "You don't have to die to see God." I asked for further explanation. Then he said, with a plainspoken honesty that I could feel vibrating over my skin, "God was there every time I saw the sun set. He was there whenever I heard a baby giggle. He was there every morning when I woke up and put my feet on the ground." The way he phrased this sounded so simple and beautiful that I thought I was chatting with an evolved and enlightened soul—a man who appreciated his every breathing moment, his kind and loving family, the very ground on which he walked.

Jim's widow and daughters were stunned. They wondered if I had the right Jim. Their father and husband, they said, was an emotionally abusive alcoholic who over the past decades had rarely had a sober day. I felt rattled, disoriented. *Did I have the right Jim?* I was in his tidy house, I could feel him, he was hovering close to his family. I had to probe further. I asked Jim why no one in his family had witnessed his close appreciation of God. A flood of remorse washed through me—Jim's remorse. He explained that when he lived in the flesh, he hadn't been aware of his meetings with God. When he transitioned from the three-dimensional world to the spirit world, loving angels came to him and showed him the story of the life he had just lived. They showed him the gifts he had received through the love and grace of God: his children, a wife who stuck by him, food in his belly each evening.

And then, as the vibrations inside me perfectly matched Jim's, he flashed into my mind's eye the same movies the angels had shown him. I narrated these movies for his family as quickly as they were coming through. (Movies that play in my head are a fairly common way for the spirit world to communicate through me; this is one of the ways I can read messages from spirits who speak a different language than I do in the three-dimensional world.)

I vividly saw the night Jim drove home drunk and, to avoid hitting a woman who was crossing the street, he swerved toward a telephone pole. I saw the speedometer at 40 mph. Jim hit that pole, and the woman walked away unharmed. He had a busted bottom lip and ended up with six stitches in his forehead. God had been there to save them both, since the time wasn't right for either of them to cross over. I also witnessed Jim in a dark alley, stumbling, tripping, and getting up again, blind drunk. He couldn't see his feet in front of him, so he surely couldn't find his way home. Once again, this unseen force enveloped him and led Jim all the way home. It was God who got him in the house and into his bed without even waking his wife. In his Earthly life, Jim was closed off and uncommunicative. But his spirit, his soul, was completely open and pure. He was an excellent communicator.

Jim's family was astonished. His widow remembered the night he drove into a telephone pole. The police called her and she rushed out to the hospital to be with him. His grown children said they often wondered how he ever made it home all those nights when they knew he was sitting in a bar somewhere, sucking down one bourbon after another. This was a faithful family who worried that Jim was going straight to Hell, where he would burn for eternity with the Devil.

During this session of spirit communication, Jim's family wept with relief. Inside that man who had made their lives so difficult was a soul full of remorse for the wasted life he'd lived on Earth, and full of love for the people he had left behind. For years this family had been trying to save Jim's soul. In the end, Divine Intervention took care of it all, bringing Jim into the light, into The God Force that surrounds us all.

And if Hell truly exists, it is right here in our tortured three-dimensional life on Earth. Together with help from the heavenly realm, and a willingness to release fears and implement forgiveness, of yourself, as well as those who have wronged you, you will be set free from the darkness that held your soul hostage. You will be freed of whatever horrors had been pulling on you during your three-dimensional life. You are freed of yourself and are now able to become one with the light of God where the only thing that matters is unconditional love.

God really is love!!!

I realize that statement can become a tautology. God is love, love is God. It's a yin-yang that circles into itself over and over again. Still, after numerous conversations with the spirit world, I think I can say it in a way that makes sense.

Love is all around us. It's energy. It's light. It actually vibrates and can be felt. The vibrations it gives off are fast and high-pitched. This vibrational energy is what we are made of. When we are our pure, authentic, original selves, we are vibrating at that high frequency with God. We are connected to the energy and light. This light, this energy, is God. We are part of God and God is part of us.

Each time we die, are reborn, and die again, we are cycling through God, through the light and vibrations, through the spirit. With each life we live on Earth, we learn lessons that help us ascend to the highest-frequency vibrations, the brightest light. This is where angels, ascended masters, and saints reside. It is what we are working toward each time we descend to Earth in order to start the process all over again.

A new birth is a clean slate, a fresh start. You'd think that if you were starting from scratch, you'd get it right the second or third time. But it takes millennia to remember that who we are is love and nothing else. And it takes work to remember this truth: to see love, to feel love, to give love, and to openly and always receive love. To be fully enlightened means to transcend the ways of the world and to vibrate at the highest Godlike frequency of pure love. And as we are in motion, moving from one dimension to the next—we are gathering emotional debris and carrying it along with us. Each of us is a giant lint filter, trapping all that spare fuzz. That fuzz, the vibrational memories of previous lives, sits in our cells, in our minds, in our souls.

Some of these memories from past lives interfere with the life you're living now. Some enrich the life you're living now. They are in you like shadows. You see them in dreams or recurring nightmares. You see them in déjà vu moments. You see them when you meet someone new who feels so familiar you could swear you've known them your whole life. Did you ever travel to somewhere totally new and feel like you'd gone home? Yup: past life. Did you ever pick up a new skill too easily, so easily it was like you'd been doing it your whole life? Yup: past life again. Did you ever witness a child do or say something that seemed completely out of time and place for that child? Children, because their past lives aren't so far in the distance, are closer to the memories of their previous lives and show them more often.

You may have come back as the thing you hated in your last life, just so you can learn to love it, learn to vibrate higher. During our three-dimensional lives, each of us must sometimes be at a low point, in darkness, so we can appreciate and feel the light. Think of Jim, the abusive alcoholic. Underneath all the booze, he was a gentle, loving soul who was only able to remember this once he lifted out of his body and was able to see himself without distractions, without filters; he was able to see clearly with his spiritual eyes. He understood the love and light of God, but only after experiencing pure despair on Earth.

The good news is that we do not have to die and leave our physical bodies, or go to the spirit world, in order to recognize love, give love, receive love, and *be* love. We were given the perfect tool at birth to allow the highest frequency known to man to filter in: love. Located right in the middle of our chests, this amazing tool is a muscle we call the heart. In spiritual circles, the heart is the gateway or energy center that allows love to flow in and out, helping us to connect the physical world with higher realms. This center is also known as the heart chakra. The heart chakra is a vibrating, spinning wheel of energy. It is responsible for giving us life while we inhabit our bodies. It is also responsible for our spiritual life, since it is through the heart that we enter enlightenment. When you allow love to flow freely through the heart, light will radiate straight from your soul and can be seen radiating through your beautiful two eyes, as I mentioned in an earlier chapter. People don't consciously realize they're seeing this light, but they are. We all are attracted to people's eyes and their radiating hearts like flies to a bug light.

When you are radiating light, people will flock to you; some of them might want something from you. Be careful, because not all flies are created equal, and some of these flies will want to feed off your light without giving up any of their own light.

If you've had significant pain, trauma, or grief in your life (and many of us have), your heart chakra might be blocked, or clogged, so that the light can't get in. Certainly, you've had your heart broken once—haven't we all? And we all know people who have a difficult or impossible time recovering from a broken heart. Going through that, you can feel an actual pulsing pain in your heart chakra. The result of this emotional blockage can result in physical ailments such as cardiac arrest or stroke. Some people have even left this Earth due to a broken heart. It probably even happened to someone you know—one half of a couple dies, and the survivor dies too, within days. These deaths are always touching, moving, and less painful for the survivors because we know that two people will be joined together in an immense, glowing love in the spirit world.

When love flows freely, you are open to connecting to and having a deep and lasting relationship with The Divine. Picture the heart as a wireless router, one with a bandwidth way bigger than 5G. Once activated, the heart chakra connects dominantly to and uses the right side of your brain as the conduit to the higher spiritual realms where only love resides. There are so many aphorisms about love: *Love makes the world go 'round, love is the answer, love will find a way, love is the key . . .* Think of all the poems, books, and songs written about love. And then there are paintings, sculptures, movies, and TV shows! It's a story told over and over again, through every possible medium. And it's a story we never grow tired of, no matter how long we've been hanging around in our three-dimensional body. Love is the glue that connects us. It has ensured the reproduction of and longevity of the human species.

This little four-letter word L-O-V-E can, and does, affect your brain. The love I felt after each of my sons was born almost blew my mind. I had thought I loved my husband more than everything—and I do—but I didn't realize that this love could grow the way it did when each of my sons came into my life. And I didn't love my husband less when the boys were born. I loved him more for being part, along with The God Force, of bringing them to me. It was a love that made me feel like something new in my head and heart had been cracked open.

Studies have shown that when a person has love in their heart, the brain is flooded with hormones such as dopamine and serotonin. And when those feel-good hormones are abundant, the part of the brain that is responsible for negative emotions such as depression and fear shuts down. Scans of the human brain have found that when a person falls in love, the frontal cortex, which is the area that is responsible for criticizing and judging, also shuts down. We've all heard the phrase "blinded by love." Well, you are certainly blinded by love when you first fall in love.

Love is our birthright. The power of love cannot be rationalized by the human brain, but it is always understood by the soul; in fact, love is the language of the soul. The language of love shows up in many ways: It can arrive as a gift on your doorstep, a feeling in your heart, a whisper in your ear, or an act of kindness. There are many ways that people have adopted to show their love to one another. Whatever form it takes, love is eternal and is what happiness is made of. It transforms obstacles into opportunities. Love is what miracles are made of. When love shows up for you, The Universe is reminding you of how lovable you are. Please do not ignore its presence; take action and answer its call.

As I said before, I had a more acute understanding of the enormous love that was emanating from my parents' hearts after experiencing the fear that was brought on me by The Gang. Contrast, the **Law of Polarity,** is what allows us to see, metaphorically and physically. If there were only blinding light in the world, you couldn't see any better than if you were surrounded by complete darkness. Love can't exist without fear. Light can't exist without darkness. It's as simple as that. As I previously mentioned, the **Law of Polarity** states that everything is defined by its opposite. The yin-yang symbol that is so popular today represents this law perfectly. One side of this symbol is black and the other side is white: the positive and the negative. Both, however, fit perfectly together like two pieces of a puzzle. Together they represent the whole. When you understand this, when you understand polarity, it allows you to stand back and look at the complete picture.

To flow with the higher frequencies, you need to surrender to the flow of life. Flowing takes you along the path of light. Struggle keeps you in resistance and takes you along the path of darkness. Even when you're flowing with the light, the darkness is present. Accepting its existence, along with accepting dips into the darkness, will help you find balance within the spectrum. And when you are balanced, living in peace and harmony, you are able to surrender to love.

Your job, as a human in the three-dimensional world, is to release all the darkness and heaviness you carry with you and to reach for the highest frequency in the realm of vibrations: love!

ALLOWING THE EGO TO DIE SO YOU CAN LIVE

Now, maybe you're saying to me, *Kim, if God is love, and love is God, and God is everywhere, why are things so messed up?!* Think back to the **Law of Polarity.** If there is love, there is also its opposite. And the opposite of love is fear. When you walk into a dark room, it is only dark until you turn on the light. When people are living in darkness, it's because they keep forgetting to turn on the light. Living in darkness is equal to living in fear, and *this* is why things are sometimes so messed up.

The energy of fear vibrates at the lowest frequency. (You'll learn more about frequencies in the next chapter.) Fear is what you go through to learn all the lessons that bring you to pure, high-vibrating God love. As I mentioned before, everything in your life is either fear-based or love-based. When you believe and do things that are love-based, you are moving toward the light, you're evolving. When you believe and do things that are fear-based, you're either stuck in a toxic soup of low-vibrational frequencies, or moving even lower toward the depths of darkness; you're dragging yourself down and dropping your soul away from love. The downward spiral is very real and the only way to get out of it is by monitoring each thought you have in the course of a day. Start off by examining the thoughts that make you feel sad or uncomfortable—ask yourself if this thought is even real and will it matter in a year from now. Does this thought hold any validity, or is it something that will most likely never even happen? As you examine each thought, try and trace it back to its origin. Perhaps it is rooted in one of those fear-based thoughts that you were programmed to believe at an early age. For example: If I let go of a relationship, I will be alone for the rest of my life. This is a total lie. Remember, you are now the adult and are able to be your own authority. You no longer have to play by other people's rules. Think new thoughts, and make sure they are positive ones. In fact, there is good news: Studies have shown that 85 percent of what we worry about never happens. Wow—that's a pretty high percentage.

To this point, the emotion of fear is the ego's most valuable tool. We all know people we'd call narcissists or egomaniacs; they're on the extreme end of the spectrum. They're living in the hell of full-blown ego fear. But, really, there's ego in all of us. Ego-based actions and decisions are actually fear-based actions and decisions.

Let's look at ego in its simplest form. What is the man who spends a month's salary on hair plugs doing? He's trying to alleviate the fear of not appearing virile, or handsome. What is going on with the woman who will no longer wear a bathing suit on the beach? Ego? Yes, because ego is fear. She is afraid of being judged. She is afraid of being mocked for the cellulite on the backs of her legs. (Believe me, I have these same fears!) What's going on with the 18-year-old boy who smokes pot all day, fails his classes, and doesn't finish a single college application? He's acting on his fear of failure. He's pretending that he's too cool for school, too unconventional to go to the same college as his parents. Really, he's afraid of his own intelligence, afraid to find out who he really is.

Conversely, let's look at the girl who really wants to go to cooking school in France and learn how to make sausages, but instead enrolls at a four-year university and studies political science because her mother's a lawyer and she's given in to her parents' conditioning: She believes she should end up as a lawyer too. Another fear-based action. Sometimes the people who look to us like they're succeeding are really failing. Failing because they're not living up to their soul's expectations of love (God) and instead are driven by their ego (fear).

Although we all uphold a certain image that we project into the world; in projecting our image, we need to be careful to pull the energy from our Higher Selves, which seek to serve humanity, rather than pulling the energy generated from our immature egos, whose only mission is to serve themselves. This is a sure way to remain in fear, forfeiting all of our personal power and surrendering it to others who have learned how to manipulate and control the masses by trusting in their own inflated egos.

Let's look at more fear-based actions. My friend Lucy works in finance and has a boss who rages. When they lose an account, he screams, bellows, and calls her names, no matter what part she had in the deal. Lucy says he stomps around the meeting room, stopping to slam his fist on the giant table. When he storms down the halls she thinks of Napoleon leading an army of just himself. "This guy," Lucy told me, "isn't afraid of anything!"

I explained to Lucy that the guy only *looks like* he's not afraid of anything. Rage, anger, and temper tantrums are three very low-vibrating energies—they are direct expressions of fear. The boss who's huffing and puffing is afraid he's lost control. Or maybe he's afraid he never had control. When he slams his fist on the table or stomps down the hall, he's afraid that no one is listening to him, that he's failed to run his own ship. The loudest way to drown out feelings of fear is through expressions of rage. Ragers run on a very low frequency, just as depressed people do. In fact, these are often the same people. Depression is another extension of fear, though sometimes it is less active than rage. We all have had times in our lives when we had a fear of taking action. Or a fear of feeling what we genuinely felt. These are related to the fear of changing our circumstances. And the biggest fear for many is the fear of being ourselves.

Loneliness is another extension of fear. The world is full of people, full of souls, and so many of them are emitting so much love. Loneliness is a way to hide from the love that's out there. It's painful. I've been lonely—it's one of the worst, most unsettling emotions. But if you can look at the fear that drives your loneliness, you can crawl out of that low frequency and move toward the higher frequency of The God Force. You are never alone when you understand that you are always connected to God. If you are connected to God, and I am connected to God, then we are connected to each other.

Of course, no one vibrates at the same frequency all the time. Even Lucy's raging boss has times when he vibrates at a higher frequency. Within a single day, your frequency is likely to change quite often. When you're fully involved in your work, and enjoying what you're doing, you're probably vibrating at a steady, medium-high frequency. If you leave work, get in your car, and drive straight into traffic, road work, detours, backups, and tolls, your frequency—depending on how you respond to this kind of stuff—will drop. When you walk into your home, depending on who you first see, your frequency might rise again, or drop lower. Just laughing and hugging someone can raise your frequency. Smiling will, too.

Please take a moment to look at the vibrational charts shown on the next page. Each emotion listed is connected to a sliding scale of vibrations that range from highest to lowest. The energy of emotions translates into real vibrations that can be measured by vibrational meters. These vibrations reside in, and are derived from, spinning wheels of lights located inside your body called energy centers or chakras. I will discuss chakras further in the next chapter.

By referring to the vibrational charts, see if you can track your frequency for today, or think about your whole week, or your month: Where has your frequency been landing? What if you take a lifetime view? Where is your set point—where does your frequency usually land? Knowing your frequency is another way to know yourself. And when you know yourself, you can unstick yourself from patterns and behaviors that hold you back from vibrating at the higher end of the vibrational chart.

Love is God. Fear is Hell. When you enter the spirit world you can choose to remain in the same consciousness you were in on Earth, or rise out of your fear and join the fearless light of God. Jim, the alcoholic whose family thought he was going to Hell, had already been living in Hell every day with his fear. He was fearful of loving and being loved. He was afraid of who he was when he was sober. He was afraid of simply living in the three-dimensional world. After viewing the "movie" of his life with the angels on the other side, Jim chose to move toward the light, toward a higher frequency.

As with Jim, angels and guides meet up with you moments after you've passed on. They go over your last life with you, talking over what happened and how you behaved. It's like a performance review, except you can't get fired and you won't get a raise. These guides will always encourage you to let go of fear, embrace all the love there is, and move toward the light, the higher frequency. But you still have free will in the spirit world. You can choose to stay at a point of stasis, hanging on to fear and the many ways it manifested in the three-dimensional world.

As an adult, I realized that The Gang who visited me when I was a child was made up of spirits who had chosen to hover on Earth and dwell in the fear they'd been living in. They were vibrating at a low, fearful frequency. This is why I was so fearful when I was near them: I was feeling their frequency, feeling their emotions.

When you reach a level of consciousness that transcends the world and all its fears, you will be bathed in the beautiful, shining light of God. In that space with God there is no fear, no shame, no ego. You will feel as if you'd been lingering in a pitch-black room and had finally flipped on the light. You can suddenly see everything clearly: love, in its pure, Godly perfection.

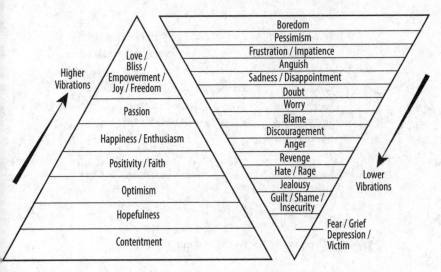

Here's a short exercise to help you identify whether you are living in a low frequency, in fear, or in a high frequency, in love. Simply seeing where you are will help you let go of your fear so that you can live your life fully washed in the light of The God Force.

Soul Search

LOVE VS. FEAR

1. List the five things you most fear and rank them from 1 to 5. Do you dwell in life's fears: poverty, illness, addiction, homelessness, or being alone? Or do you dwell in social fears: parties, dating, public speaking, work performance, job interviews? Or are your fears personally tuned to what you think of as you: elevators, dentist visits, crowded movie theaters?

2. Do you often or ever think about death? How do you feel about death? Describe the emotions that come up as you write your answer.

3. Draw four concentric circles, one inside the other—a bull's-eye. In the center circle, list the people to whom you are closest, the people you feel you can't live without. On the next circle, put people who don't make it into that closest circle but who you think of as good friends. Work your way out to neighbors or acquaintances.

4. To use a familiar metaphor, do you tend to look at the glass as half empty or half full?

Let's look at your answers to these simple questions.

Question 1: Are the fears you listed controlling or influencing your life? Are your moods or actions directly associated with these fears? Next to each fear, write what would happen if you let go of the fear. What in your daily life would change if this fear had no influence on how you lived your daily life? What would happen if you let go of trying to control your fears and how you respond to them and, instead, put them in the hands of The Universe? Try it for one minute. Then for one hour. See how your mood, your vibrational frequency, changes.

Question 2: If you're preoccupied with death, as many people are, ask yourself how these thoughts change your day, or your mood? Do you have questions about death; does it feel unknown and beyond your control? Write down every question you have about death. Hopefully, by the end of this book, those questions will be answered and you will feel more comfortable with the spiritual cycle. Trust that death is not an end point—rather it's a passage.

Question 3: Look at the people in your innermost circle. Do you trust them? Do you feel enveloped in love when you're with them? Ask yourself this of each of the people in each of the circles. When you surround yourself with people you love who love you back, you raise your vibrational frequency toward the light, toward The God Force. When your frequency is raised, you attract others with high frequencies. Likewise, low frequencies attract low-frequency people. This is the **Law of Attraction.** See if you can arrange your life, and use your time in the three-dimensional world, so that you are mostly surrounded by high-frequency people. Although it's true you can't avoid certain people such as family members or coworkers, try your best not to allow yourself to become the victim of their drama. As I often say, "shut it down," or "pull the plug"—which means eliminate the power that fuels their drama, aka their ego. Walk away or be blunt and tell them it's not your circus and not your monkeys—a fun phrase to remember when trying to lighten the mood. It is also true that low-vibrational people may get angry when they lose their audience, but don't let that bother you for even one second. These people are very capable of quickly finding an entire new crowd to dump their garbage on. When you release low-frequency people, you spring toward the higher vibrations, toward the light where you are surrounded with love. You weren't born to linger in the darkness; you were born to love and to give love. After all, *you are love!*

Question 4: If you go through the steps outlined in the responses to questions 1, 2, and 3, you might be able to turn your gaze away from darkness and toward the light. I know it's not easy to change habits. And even our moods become habits! But if you've identified yourself as someone who is operating on a low frequency, then you are ready to leave behind your fears and leap toward the relief of a higher frequency. Practice this by flipping your point of view. Each time you see something in the negative, or through the emotion of fear, flip it in your mind and look at it through the lens of love. See what happens when you do this over and over again. Chances are, you'll create a new habit—a better one, you'll raise your vibrational frequency and move closer to the light of God.

SOUL KIT

Meditation for Releasing Fear

Here's another meditation. (I can't overstate the value of meditating!) Each time you feel your frequency lowering, or feel yourself turning toward the shadow side or a lower chakra, repeat the following phrase in your mind five times as you breathe in deeply through your nose and out your mouth: *I breathe in love, I breathe out fear. I breathe in love, I breathe out fear.*

Do you remember that soup of vibrational energy that we're all swimming in, the electrical soup that connects us to one another and to The God Force? When you push energy to one place, you eliminate energy from another: That's the **Law of Balance** in action. When you breathe in love, you open your heart chakra—and an open heart chakra filled with love increases your vibrational frequency. And when you increase your frequency, fear is pushed away. Amazing that you can take care of all this simply by breathing.

5

What's Your Vibe? Mastering Vibrational Frequencies and Understanding Chakras

> *"Your vision will become clear, only when you look into your heart. Who looks outside dreams, who looks inside, awakens."*
>
> —CARL JUNG

WHEN THE Beach Boys sang about good vibrations over half a century ago, they might not have realized how dead-on they were. Though maybe they did, since music—like all the arts, like all creative activity—taps into and emerges from your soul.

In this chapter we're going to dig deeper into those vibrations. We're going to look at how all living things, and all nonliving things too, are essentially made up of vibrations. We'll also learn *why* those vibrations are important to us.

When I talk to spirits I am feeling the energy, the vibrations, from a particular soul. That energy generates signals creating symbols in my mind, which I then translate to words. Yes, there are other ways I talk to spirits. In my first book, I told you about my dear husband, who sleeps through the most exciting moments in my life, when the spirits talk to me through his mumbling somnambulistic voice while he's out cold. It's like a party at his house that he's never able to attend and only gets to hear about after the fact.

Now here's the thing about reading vibrations: everyone can do it, not just mediums and psychics. In fact, you probably already do it without thinking about it. Each time you meet with a person, or enter a room with people already in it, you feel *something*, right? You walk into a movie theater for a matinee and there's that one guy sitting in the front row and a couple sitting in the back row. All the other seats are empty. There's a vibe in that 2:00 p.m. showing where only the four of you have paid the money to watch it. You probably don't want to stay in the theater. The guy in the front row might be angry and lonely— the energy he's giving off, his vibrations, is saying, *Go away.* The young couple in the back, they want to focus on each other. They're swirling in a soup of their own vibrations and are likely saying, *Leave us alone.*

And then there are places where you get happy vibes, or energetic vibes. When you pick your daughter up from kindergarten on the day they went to the petting zoo and she touched a real, live goat! The vibe in that room is happy, excited, optimistic. Those five-year-olds are shooting off high vibrations that infiltrate your skin and go deep inside you. You can't help but feel it too.

Even on the phone you get vibes. Ever get that call from a friend who likes to complain about nothing? She groans about the fact that the hot sauce she likes is no longer being carried at Gristedes, the shoes she took to get repaired aren't ready yet, her closet is too crowded, and she hates all her clothes. Yes, we all have that friend. Her vibe is low, and slow. Let's say you're in your car when you take her call. I'm pretty sure you'll tell her that you've arrived at your destination way before you've even reached the turnoff. As soon as you hang up from her, your friend Sam calls. He's written a musical that's going to be playing on Broadway using all the songs from the Go-Go's. He is thrilled. His creative work is about to shine on a big stage. His vibration is so high, you're about to pop through the sunroof of your car when you've got him on the phone. Sam is oozing excitement, creating good vibrations.

You've probably already noticed, too, that vibrations are contagious. When you finish the phone call with your friend who complains about the shape of ice cubes, your own vibration has dropped. We do that as humans—we match our vibrations to others. But Sam's phone call may have saved you. With him chattering on the phone, practically screaming with joy, your vibration lifted, sped up, to match his.

Some people spread their vibrations more than others—they spray them out like skunks. In my house, growing up, it was my dad. Whatever mood he was in when he came home from work was the mood of the whole house. Even my sweet cousin Mary, if she came over from next door, with her usually happy, high vibes, she couldn't help but have them plummet to my dad's low ones. For my friend Bella, it was her mother whose vibrations dictated the tone of the house. Bella's mom's vibrations changed radically from day to day. After school, Bella would enter the house hesitantly, waiting to see what kind of vibe she was coming home to. When her mom was happy, radiating high vibrations, Bella's vibrations soared. They'd put on music and dance together while they made dinner for the rest of the family. When her mom was depressed or angry, Bella's vibrations sank like the Titanic. She felt like she was closing up like a cardboard box, getting darker and lower each minute she was alone with her mother. Bella couldn't wait for her little brother and sister to come home with their energy and excitement. They didn't tune in to the mother as much as Bella did, and they changed the vibrations rather than reacting to others'.

My readings, when I'm in the season of doing them, are scheduled back to back. Because I'm making connections with souls in the spirit world, I'm usually working with the bereaved, people who feel as though their hearts have been ripped straight from their chests. The ones who lost children don't even know how to continue with their lives. My heart breaks for each and every one of these people. Now, my gift, as you know, directs me to read vibrations. But not just those of departed souls; I also read the vibrations of the living.

As you can imagine, people at the lowest point in their lives are existing with very low vibrations—I mean, vibrations that feel like they're coming from a bottomless trench. This presents a problem, because in order to connect with those who have passed on, I need to bring my vibrations up to a higher level than even someone who's having a great day. In order to pull off this feat of interacting with someone at the lowest vibrations and raising my vibrations, I have to almost shield myself from the lower vibrations of the bereaved, while also pulling from a store of high vibrations within me. Otherwise, my own vibrations would plummet. (Remember the **Law of Attraction:** *Like attracts like.*)

My spirit guides, in collusion with my husband, who books my appointments, are always looking out for me, though. They usually alternate my low-vibrational clients with high-vibrational clients. This allows me a little reprieve and gives me the time to re-up my own frequency. Those who conduct readings know exactly what I'm talking about. I'm sure that psychiatrists, doctors, nurses, and funeral directors know what I'm talking about too. They don't talk to souls, but they certainly have to interact with people with extremely low vibrations that would drag them down if they're not careful.

Let's look closer at these vibrations, so we can understand their range and frequency. I like to use a scale that runs from 1 to 22 (see chart on page 67). It's easy to grasp and easy to find your place on the scale. (Some people use scales that go to 1,000, but who wants to sit around and wonder where you are between 750 and 869—769? No, wait, 803? You get the picture.) To name the two ends, I'm going to give you two words that describe the sum of all your emotions, of all the emotion in the universe: love and fear. Fear is at the bottom of the scale—it's 22. Love is at the top—it's 1.

Believe me, I can hear all of you chattering out there. You're telling me, *Kim, I've got about 3,000 emotions beyond love and fear. I've experienced 2,000 of them already on my train ride into the city this morning!* Yes, you may have experienced a variety of emotions on the train this morning. You were angry when the train was late. You were frustrated when you stepped in that puddle that may not have been water, right before you stepped on the train. You were irritated that you didn't get a seat. You were disgusted with the guy who took the seat right in front of you, who cleared his throat incessantly during the whole ride. You were outraged that it started raining by the time you got to your destination, and getting a cab was impossible. You were kicking yourself for not having thought to bring an umbrella this morning. And then, when you finally arrived at the office, you were exhausted and fed up.

I get what you're saying. That's a lot of emotion for one morning. A lot of emotion for one person to carry—and none of it you'd label fear.

But remember, the emotion that is coming out of you at a particular moment might not be fear, but it originates in fear.

The simplest way to look at it is this: Anything that isn't love is working against love. Anything that works against love is fear-based.

Before we move on, let's talk briefly about the biology and physics of vibrations.

The Earth is surrounded by an electrically and magnetically charged field called the magnetic field, geomagnetic field, or magnetosphere. This energy starts in the outer core of the Earth and extends all the way into space, where it meets the charged particles of the sun, known as the solar wind. In physics, electromagnetic (EM) radiation refers to the flow of this energy at the universal speed of light through free space or through transmitters like microwaves. EM waves are measured in *hertz*, or units of frequency. There are lower frequencies like radio waves and television waves, and higher frequencies like ultraviolet rays and X-rays.

As I mentioned in an earlier chapter, everything in the universe is made up of energy, including the atoms that create our bodies. Our bodies, these energetic forces, are swimming in a soup made of the EM field that surrounds our planet. This means we are in a constant state of flowing through and being part of the magnetic radiation of the sun, the Earth, our smartphones, lightbulbs, television sets, television remotes, toasters, and so on. You might not realize this consciously, but your body understands this, just as your heart understands that it needs to keep beating to keep you alive.

Many species, ranging from bacteria to bats, read the electromagnetic fields of energy, or geo fields, through what is called *magnetoreception*. Humans don't practice magnetoreception, but there is a protein in the retina called a cryptochrome, a blue light sensor, which could serve as a magnetoreceptor, so theoretically it could be developed. (There are studies of blind people who easily move through life without a cane or a dog because they rely on other highly developed skills previously thought to exist only in animals—like the echolocation that bats use. And a professor at Caltech is conducting studies to hone magnetoreception in humans.)

Species with magnetoreception align their bodies to the magnetic field of the Earth and the light of the sun. This allows them to understand where they are and where they want to go on the planet. Birds, sea turtles, and butterflies all use magnetoreceptors activated by the cryptochromes in their retinas. Along with their normal aerial view, it is believed that migrating birds look at magnetic fields as an overlay on the Earth—like something you might see on the screen of a video game where you're pretending to fly a plane.

Even plants contain cryptochromes, though obviously plants don't have eyes, so they're not in their retinas. Plants will grow according to the amount of light sensed, or processed, through the cryptochrome. Whether or not plants sense the electromagnetic field is being studied but is yet to be fully understood.

Though we are not exactly like butterflies, birds, homing pigeons, or pea plants, we are connected to them just as we are connected to each other. To think of yourself as an individual separate from everything else in The Universe is like thinking of a star that is separate from the sky: impossible. The God Force, all the energy in The Universe, is like a giant web in which we are all tangled. If I pull my arm back, it changes the energy around me, which changes the flight of a butterfly in Africa. Usually we hear a version of this in the reverse: *If a butterfly flaps its wings* . . . It might help you understand your interconnectedness to all things, all beings, all spirits, all souls.

When you flap your arms you change the energy around you, and you emit energy as well. There are seven focal balls of energy inside you called your *chakras*. Each chakra emits energy at a different frequency. These frequencies have been measured and are real. The chakra that most concerns us in the search for your soul purpose is the heart chakra. Just as the heart is our most essential organ, it is the most essential chakra we must open and feed to be connected to The God Force.

We are all created by God, and what God creates first in each human is the heart—it is the initial organ to develop in an embryo. The heart chakra emits the highest, brightest frequency of any chakra. When the electrical field of the heart is measured by an electrocardiogram, it is found to be about 60 times greater in amplitude than that of the brain. How amazing is that! Your heart chakra is your center, it is part of your soul; to open it up and let love flow through it is to be connected to The God Force and The Universe in the most divine way.

It is what we are all reaching for as we work our way through this life adventure in our three-dimensional body.

In earlier text, I spoke about how grief and despair can physically affect a person's health, particularly their heart. Here I would like to elaborate on the effects of having a blocked off heart chakra. When your heart is closed off to love, you are closed off to all the great beauty in the world—being with God, being on this adventure. Operating your life with a closed heart is like trying to operate a TV with a half-power battery remote. You might be able to get the TV on, but you won't be able to change the channel to find the show you want to watch. Without a fully charged remote, you'll be stuck on one channel, and there may be signal interruptions causing static. In life, without a fully charged heart chakra, you'll be stuck, as well—stuck in a life that is not flowing and glowing with the love that is The Universe all around us.

Miracles flow through an open-heart center. Have you ever seen someone witness a miracle? What do they do? They put their hands on their heart, one atop the other. The body knows. The hands know. You know these truths in your intuitive self. But in order to create and see the miracles that are out there, you need to open your heart.

It's a small, rugged, hard existence without an open heart. Remember the Grinch? His little peach pit of a heart did him no good. But as soon as his heart opened, the world changed for him. All that singing, glory, and good was there all along, just as it is there all along for you and me. The answer is to *see the love and the good that is already surrounding you.* But in order to see it, you have to open your heart chakra, allowing it to flow with its great electrical charge. Just as, in order to channel surf all the shows on TV, you have to put fresh batteries in your remote!

A closed heart is blind to love and to God. When your heart chakra is closed energy is pushed out of the lower chakras. I spoke at length about chakras in my first book, *The Happy Medium,* so I just want to touch on them briefly here.

There are seven chakras in the human body. Chakras are spinning wheels of energy made up of cosmic light that run up and down your spine from your pelvis to the crown of your head. They are similar to rechargeable batteries and serve as energy portals for the human body; cosmic energy and light are pulled in from the atmosphere, flowing in and out of them connecting the physical body with the spiritual realms. This flow allows each chakra to spin in a certain direction. When one chakra is blocked and out of whack, it affects the spinning motion of the other chakras (the **Law of Balance**). When these energy centers all spin in alignment, then each chakra is considered to be open (balanced) and healthy. Problems occur when the stresses of life creep in. Stress, along with negative emotions that we refuse to let go of, clog these spinning wheels of light and energy, slowing them down or leaving them stagnant or blocked. When a chakra is blocked, less energy and light are present and we experience the shadow side of its function. This shadow side connects to ideas and actions that can lead us away from our soul purpose. When we push the envelope and ignore the warning signs, ultimately, we live out of the shadow side of our chakras, resulting in many imbalances in our whole system, both physical and emotional.

The chakras below the heart are called lower chakras; these chakras are where the underdeveloped ego dwells and is connected to the three-dimensional world. As we learned, if not tamed, the ego could wreak havoc in our lives by convincing us of many lies rooted in fear. The chakras that sit at the heart and above are called the higher chakras and are connected to The Divine, or love. These higher chakras connect to the higher or heavenly realms where we are able to connect to the Ascended Masters and God. Each chakra has a color that it emits, creating an aura that surrounds your body. Starting with your first chakra, red is located at the bottom or your pelvis, and is connected to your root. The second chakra is orange, and is located directly below your navel and is called your sacral chakra. The third chakra is yellow, and is located right above your navel and is called your solar plexus. The fourth chakra is green and is located in the center of your chest right where your heart is and is called your heart chakra. The fifth chakra is blue or turquoise, and is located at your throat area and likewise it is known as the throat chakra. The sixth chakra is the color indigo (a combination of blue and red) and is located in the center of your forehead; this chakra is called the third eye, or the brow chakra. And finally, the seventh chakra is violet, often mixed with white, and is located at the top of your head, connected to your crown ,and is called the crown chakra. See diagram on the following page.

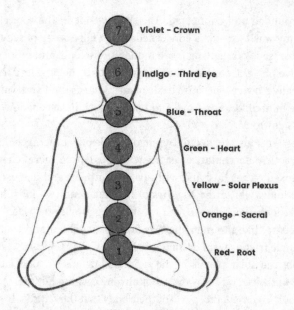

Let me tell you about my friend Amy. Like many of us (and I don't exclude myself from anything we discuss), Amy likes to watch reality television. I'm sure that many of the men and women in reality shows are kind, good, loving people. I'm not talking about any of them in particular. But the way these shows are edited and broadcast places undue value on the shadow side of the lower chakras. There is much drama and focus on material goods, greed, competition, superficial beauty, jealousy, anger, resentments, revenge. You name it—reality TV has an episode revolving around it. Amy, who is beautiful inside and out, thought her life wasn't glamorous enough. She didn't think she was pretty *enough*, she didn't think her lips were puffy *enough*, she didn't think her hair was long *enough*, she didn't think her clothes were fancy *enough*, she didn't think her house was impressive *enough*, and she didn't think her marriage was sexy *enough*. So what did this woman—who I swear to you is a very intelligent and good person—do? Well, she started with Botox, moved on to fillers, had a facelift and enlarged her breasts, divorced her husband, sold the house, and moved to a town where she thought she would meet a richer man.

Amy lived out of, and acted on, the shadow side of all seven chakras. The lowest chakra is the root chakra, which is good for feeling grounded and connected. The shadow side of the root chakra, where Amy was focused, is concerned with a false sense of security. She was obsessed with getting more money, more food, and more goods. In the caveman era, our root chakras served us by helping us survive—I mean really survive—because basic needs, such as food and water, needed to be hunted for. For Amy, and people stuck in the shadow of their root, it's gluttony.

Amy also turned to the shadow side of her sacral chakra. Instead of practicing acceptance, as one with a balanced sacral chakra does, she looked at her husband with disappointment and disgust. She wanted to know why, after 20 years of marriage and two kids, he didn't look like a soap opera star who was earning movie star wages. Why wasn't he sexy like the men she was fantasizing about and that some of her single friends were dating?

The solar plexus is the next chakra up. It's associated with self-confidence and self-worth. But anyone cashing out their retirement account to exaggerate parts of their body that they think are going to draw people to them (rather than using their great intelligence, charm, or wit) is not living with self-confidence or self-worth. I am all for improving what God gave us through methods of modern technology and by using certain beauty products, but again, remembering the **Law of Balance** is key. Amy's solar plexus was anything but balanced; it was completely out of whack, leaving her to face the shadow side of this chakra.

The heart chakra is all about love, joy, compassion, charity, inner peace, and connecting to The God Force. And though Amy has tremendous love for her grown children, her friends, and her family, much of that love was obscured because she was living out of the shadow side of her heart. By now, you should know what the opposite of love is, right? Yes, fear! Fear of aging, fear of being unattractive, fear of losing sexuality and potency, fear of being ignored while growing older, fear of marrying—do I need to go on?

The throat chakra, which is associated with expressing oneself truthfully, was certainly closed off in Amy. What truth is there in thinking that a better zip code will make you a better person or will help you find a better person to love you?

The third eye chakra is about gaining wisdom and the ability to see the big picture, see your place in The Universe. The opposite of truth is illusion. And though Amy is normally not a delusional person, when she acted out of so much fear, her actions ended up harming many people, not just herself.

Amy's crown chakra, which when balanced and open, represents an unlimited amount of cosmic goodness, including an inner beauty that shines, unconditional love, and connecting to The Divine. This certainly wasn't the case for Amy, and her crown was everything but shiny. The shadow side of this chakra is represented by separation, and a lack of empathy. Surely in time, Amy will feel the effects of being isolated from her team of supporters, and depression is sure to set in. Eventually, Amy will feel the negative effects of her decisions and will hopefully let go of her fear-based perceptions

The false identity of the ego, which is singular and totally driven by the lower chakras, helps no one; it doesn't even help the person to whom it belongs. When you make ego-based decisions, you might falsely believe that you are making your life better. In truth, ego-based decisions only serve the ego, which is not a part of the soul or your soul purpose.

So, instead of submitting to the joy and goodness of The Universe and The God Force, Amy put all her focus and energy into her ego and the shadow side of all seven chakras. And where did that land her? Ego tries to compete with us and almost always convinces us that we should stand alone, apart from one another and from God. Ego-based actions never serve the soul. And when you don't serve your soul, you move farther from your soul purpose.

Well, in the end, just as I suspected, Amy's finances are in shambles after the divorce; she's lonely and misses her husband; her grown children won't speak to her; and she's sitting alone in a half-empty rental trying to eat a microwaved dinner with lips that have a residual numbness, as if she just got out of dental surgery. I know she'll pull through and return to the light, to The God Force, to opening up her heart chakra to all that is good. But for now, she is stuck in the low vibrations of negative energy, negative desires, and pursuits that have no value in the spirit world. Amy wants to date a "great" guy, she tells me on the phone. But like attracts like when it comes to energy. And with all that energy coming out of her shadow side, the only men she's attracted to are ones who are living in equally low vibrations.

If you want to change the people you draw, you need to change your own vibrations first. In other words, no one with an open heart and spirit will come to Amy until she herself has opened her heart and spirit to what really matters. Ego-based actions vibrate at a low frequency. Heart chakra–based actions vibrate at a high frequency.

You may have heard the saying "Your vibe attracts your tribe." Rather than calling it a tribe, I like to view it more like a team. Each person on a team plays a different role in helping one another achieve a desired goal. I would prefer to have people on my team who accentuate the positive mindset. As I mentioned before, every once in a while, we will be faced with negative people whom we can't avoid—people who emit vibes at lower frequencies. It is important to be aware of these frequencies and learn not to lower your own frequency just to appease these Debbie Downers. People who stay on the lower end of the frequency scale are usually surrounded by other people who emit a frequency similar to theirs—this is clearly when we can witness the **Law of Attraction** in action. In other words, when you lie with dogs, you get fleas. When you vibrate at a high frequency and draw other high-frequency people to you, you find the people who truly get you and who you admire.

Admiration is inspiration. Jealousy is a negative form of admiration, a low-vibrating way that makes you feel competitive. But to admire someone, to praise them for how they live, act, create, and give to the community, is to aspire to be like them. When you turn jealousy on its head, you look at the people you want to be like through your heart chakra and not through your lower chakras. In doing this, your soul becomes closer to their soul and your vibrations match their vibrations.

Amy's heart won't open to a higher frequency until she gives up trying to control the uncontrollable—her body, aging, her finances (to a certain degree now that she's divorced)—and submits to The Higher Power. The Universe loves Amy exactly as she is—no matter what her zip code! And once she sees that, once she understands how fleeting this adventure in this three-dimensional life is, she'll see how misplaced her energy has been. She will finally see her divine expression of true beauty.

Soul Search

WHAT'S YOUR VIBE?

1. If pure love is at level 1 and pure fear is at level 22, where would your average daily vibration be?

2. List the people in your inner circle. What number would you give their average frequency?

3. In a crisis, what is the role you assume? Leader? Calm one? Hysterical one? Or the inner child who needs to be cared for?

4. Explain how you'd handle the following situation. (Rework the dynamics if you must, but try to keep the scenario as high-stress as this one.) Your sister's getting married in California. You, your spouse, and your kids plan to fly out there a day early from New York to help her get ready. When you get to the airport, you find that your flight has been delayed for three hours. By the end of that time, your kids and husband are bored, grouchy, hungry, and whiny. Just when you think it's time to board, the flight is canceled altogether and you're told the next flight they can get you on is two days later, which means you'll miss your sister's wedding. Note: You are unable to find another airline to accommodate your needs. Explain exactly how you'd react.

Soul Work Day One

1. Explain this chapter to three or more people who are in your daily life. (Choose people who do not know you intimately, like your boss or a neighbor.) Ask them to rank you on a scale of 1 to 22.

2. Ask them to say what they think you'd do in the airport scenario.

3. Keep a notebook for 24 hours and make periodic notes of what you're feeling and what you think your vibe is on the scale of 1 to 22. Don't judge yourself or make excuses, just take note.

After you've completed the homework and the quiz, do the following:

1. Compare how you see yourself to how others see you. Do they match up? Are you vibrating at a lower frequency than you'd like to be? Are you surrounded by people who are also vibrating at a lower frequency? (Remember the **Law of Attraction**.)

2. Write the name of the chakra next to each emotion you noted in your journal. Indicate whether you think it was the shadow side of the chakra or you were turning toward the light, The God Force. What would you say your average frequency was for the day?

Soul Work Day Two

Keep a journal as you did the day before. This time, each time you notice yourself acting or *thinking thoughts* that vibrate from a lower chakra, or the shadow side of a chakra, say aloud the word *CANCEL*. Visualize the chakra as a ball of energy you can hold in your hand. Imagine yourself turning it so you are looking at the light side, The God Force side, the side that vibrates at a higher frequency. Learn to match a high vibration emotion to the beautiful, glowing chakra ball. I'll give you a hint. Think of a funny memory that, even to this day, puts a smile on your face. Hold this memory for a few seconds. Take a deep breath and release. There, I see you smiling. After practicing this all day, examine yourself in a meditation, then see where your vibrational frequency now lands on the chart.

SOUL KIT

As I mentioned earlier, in order to banish fear, we must bring more love into our lives. The heart chakra is responsible for our ability to love. In order to open this magnificent gateway, we must also experience sorrow and disappointment—which is different from fear. Obviously, this is not what we try to manifest, but it's part of the duality of the heart chakra—we need to feel both sides. Here are a few tips the spirit world has given me to help you to open your heart:

- Cry. Many people are taught to be brave or strong and not to cry; it is often labeled as a sign of weakness. Crying cleanses our soul and helps us release stored old emotions that weigh us down. It helps open one's heart center. Try watching a sad love story to get the tears flowing.

- Adopt a pet. Having love for a pet connects us to our hearts. Studies have shown that just taking care of and petting our animals releases feel-good hormones. Also, when you give love to your trusty new friend, they return it unconditionally.

- Become more charitable. Give more than you receive. Giving whatever we can to someone less fortunate not only allows us to have more empathy and compassion, which helps open the heart, but also helps us to feel good about ourselves, knowing we are doing our part to help in some small way. Go to a homeless shelter, animal shelter, or even a nursing home for a short visit. Just a visit or a smile can go a long way.

- Love yourself more. Loving yourself the way God loves you is one of the most powerful tools you can carry. Stop believing the lies you were taught about sacrificing your happiness in order to please others. Be true to yourself and don't have lunch with the low-frequency neighbor when you really want to work on that blanket you're knitting for your soon-to-be-born grandchild. Work your way to saying no to people and activities that bring down your vibrational frequency—instead, say yes to people and activities that are swimming in the high frequency love of The God Force.

My wish for you, dear readers, is that you will all live in a higher frequency, with well-balanced chakras, especially a shiny, glowing heart chakra. In this way, you will be connected to and basking in the glowing light of The Universe. And you'll be connected to your center, the place where you can find your soul purpose.

Find Your Team: Learn How
to Love Yourself More and Become
a Team Player

> *"If you want to travel fast, go alone.*
> *If you want to travel far, go together."*
> —N'GAMBAI TRIBE

As Disney so eloquently put it, "All your dreams can come true if you have the courage to pursue them." Easier said than done, right? We all need courage to navigate these bodies in the three-dimensional world. But where does that courage come from? Why do some people have it and others don't?

If you think of your moments of courage, they were probably moments when you felt supported, bolstered by someone or by a group of people. Courage takes strength. And courage often depends on the idea that no matter how far we fall, someone we love will come up behind us and scoop us back up to standing.

No matter how independent or self-sufficient we believe ourselves to be, the truth is that everyone needs a good support system. Sure, you can try to go at it alone, but why would you want to? A little help from the people we love can go a long way, especially when it comes to finding your soul purpose.

I would like to mention the caveman again. We can think of his simple way of living, similar to a monk's life in the mountains of Tibet. Both have the ability to sit quietly and listen to the whispers of his soul. Although I'm not sure the caveman necessarily thought about his soul—he was busy protecting his family—in living his simple life, he was closer to the soul. Now, most of us can't readily set up shop in the mountains of Tibet, but we can access these whispers, even if we live in a studio apartment in the middle of noisy New York. We too have been communally raised, and, no matter where we are, we can and usually do access our team.

After 6 million years of conditioning (130,000 years as modern man), it is in our nature to think that our community's way of doing things is the only way, or the most efficient way, to handle any given situation. We espouse our community's beliefs, politics, and point of view as the best and right way. It is often hard for us to wrap our minds around the ideas and ways of other communities, since their foreignness can seem "wrong" to us. This, of course, is the argument for diversity. Exposure to other cultures and people leads to understanding and acceptance of other cultures and people, which leads us back to the central truth of The Universe: We all are from the same source and are inescapably connected to one another through our souls, love, and The Divine.

Today, we usually learn the lay of the land through the thought patterns and behaviors of our families. In each new body we enter, this is our community and we must play by its rules. The moment you were born, you only had the interests God gave you, which were love and light. But you learned the beliefs and behaviors of your community and likely accepted them and identified with them. As an adolescent, you may have turned things around and rejected the ideas or beliefs of your community, just as I rejected going to confession at the Catholic church. Still, whether you rebelled or not, the essence of what you were rebelling against was likely the teachings of your family of origin.

We are taught community thinking through observation, family living, neighborhood living (especially if we live in a homogeneous area), education, religious training, and also punishment and shaming by any of the aforementioned groups. We learn quickly that if we wander too far from our community and adopt ways that do not fit into the communal beliefs, we will no longer be accepted. We imagine ourselves spiritually, or sometimes literally, homeless without the support of our community. And that untethered, cut-loose feeling, for most of us, is one of the scariest things there is. *Who are we, we wonder, when we are not part of this group with whom we've been raised? Who are we when there is no one to witness us?*

Have you ever noticed that no matter how far you stray from your original community, you still want your accomplishments and successes to be known by them? The impulse to be validated by that original group, even if we've left them, is a hard one to let go of. And, of course, we want our achievements to be validated by our current community too. No wonder social media exploded the way it has: There are now endless platforms on which we can be "seen" and recognized, making sure all of our communities from all the different areas of our lives can see what we're doing—or what we want them to *think* we're doing. Posting for recognition can suck up a lot of our time. It might feel good at the time, but ultimately, it doesn't replace authentic human connection. It doesn't serve our soul purpose, God's purpose, for each of us. When God made us and put us on planet Earth, His intention was for us to interact with each other and to love each other face-to-face.

In Western cultures, and the United States in particular, great value is placed on independence. We respect and admire people who "make it on their own," or who "pull themselves up by their bootstraps." We see these people, who appear to charge forward without the help of others, as resilient and strong. But does anyone ever really accomplish anything entirely on their own, or is this just a story we like to tell ourselves—a story we pretend to believe? Many of us tend to ignore the pillar of events, people, education, and The Divine that supports us and gives us the necessary courage to get to where we want to go. Even if you don't want to recognize the "group effort" in every achievement, you can't avoid the fact that if you trace any achievement back to its origin, you will be bumping into many people, as well as divine forces, that helped with the process.

The farther in geological time we move from the caveman era, the more our communities seem to be breaking apart. In the United States and Canada, kids often go off to college by leaving one coast for the other. People follow the money as they take jobs that lead them away from their family home, sometimes as far as the other side of the planet—Dubai, Hong Kong, Uganda. Technological advancements make it possible for people to work remotely. I know a guy who lives in Thailand, whose office is in New York, and whose family is in Amsterdam. This is how the modern world operates.

Little by little, we have been disconnecting from human interaction. And I'm not considering a chat while playing Words with Friends a human interaction! Even people who stay close to their hometown work in ways that isolate them from the community. Cubicles with four-foot walls do nothing to create community. We are attached to our phones and computers and do most of our communicating, even with people who are only a block away, through one apparatus or another. Admit it: You've texted someone who was only a room away when you could have walked down the hall to see them face-to-face. My friend Allison texted her husband the other day from their king-size bed, *while he was in the bed with her.* Imagine that!

Each modern convenience of the world, along with our addiction to social media, only seems to make our work days longer and more demanding. By the time we get home, we're often too exhausted to cook dinner. And if no one cooks dinner, how does a family sit down and eat together? Study after study has shown that one of the most important things you can do for the development and well-being of your children is to sit down and eat dinner with them. Only one generation ago, it was unimaginable that a family wouldn't sit down together for dinner every night. But progress, along with inflation and the high cost of living (many people need two jobs just to pay the rent) has led us away from the behaviors we've lived with for as long as we've been on the planet. Even our enormous houses separate families (think of my friend Allison, texting her husband in bed), whereas it wasn't long ago that families huddled together in one room to sleep. (I've gotta admit here that I wouldn't exchange my king-size bed for all the tea in China!)

We're stuck in a cycle of buying, consuming, and then desperately laboring to make money to pay for the things we've bought. Other than food and shelter, few of these purchases sustain us in any meaningful way. At the end of a hard workday, we fall into bed exhausted, only to wake up a few short hours later so we can do it all over again. Remember the movie *Groundhog Day*, where Bill Murray woke up to live the same day over and over again? Most of us connected to that film because in our work/spend/work cycle, we feel like we're living a version of Groundhog Day. We spend all week looking forward to the weekend, when we plan to catch up on sleep, watch a movie, maybe eat a leisurely dinner. But how many times has your weekend been sucked away in the tunnel of chores you never got around to doing during the week?

When we live our lives this way, we don't have time to create new adventures and make new memories. Yes, memories. Few people reflect on their previous life and think about how amazing it was to sit at a desk entering 150 email addresses into an Excel spreadsheet. You reflect and think about the times you were with people, doing interesting things, seeing new places, laughing, eating, *connecting*! These were the things that used to come naturally, that used to be part of our everyday life. Now times like that are planned, penciled in on a calendar, only to be erased if something big comes up at work. Unfortunately, this isolation and Groundhog Day living doesn't serve God's purpose. And when you think about it, it doesn't feed our purpose either, and it definitely doesn't feed our souls.

When I was growing up, my maternal grandmother lived with us. All my aunts, uncles, and cousins (some of whom lived next door) frequently came to our house to visit Nanny. Because she was there—the leader of my family—our house was a central gathering place for dozens of people. Both my mother and my Nanny loved to cook, so there was always plenty of food, enough for growing boys and girls and enormous uncles who loved to eat. There was joking, storytelling, playing cards, and lots and lots of laughter. On some occasions, the belly laughs were so intense, some family members would have to change their pants. (I won't give up any names!) The family fed us. The family entertained us. The family nourished us emotionally.

Of course, there were disagreements and arguments (some that I still remember). And of course, I'm sure there were dark things going on behind the scenes that I simply didn't know about. But even when we weren't getting along, we all knew that family came first. When I get together with my family today, it always raises my frequency or vibration, just as it did when I was a kid. I could always feel the vibrations of happiness and love in my home, and surely everyone else did too. In this way, the need of every soul in my family to love and be loved was met. And that, my friends, is something that money can never buy.

For humans, love and connection is as essential to growth and development as food and vitamins. As I said before, a child who doesn't bond to another human suffers terribly, emotionally and physically, as he grows. To be deprived of love is a form of torture. Solitary confinement in prisons has been proved to do great psychological harm to those it's inflicted on. In fact, all primates need love and bonding to thrive. Look at the study Harry Harlow did with monkeys in the 1950s: Separated from their mothers, baby monkeys snuggled and sought love from a wood-and-fabric monkey placed in their cage. The monkeys who were given a hard, wire "mother" could not function well in times of stress. They had no core of love to which they could retreat, no community to give them the courage to exist in the complications of a three-dimensional body.

Our work/spend/work cycle does not, and will never, satisfy our most basic human needs. Even after we have beauty, power, and money, we will remain unsatisfied, itchy, unsettled. Many people respond to this feeling by seeking more money, more power, more beauty. But nothing will satisfy the person who seeks these things, for these are not our essential needs—they do not feed our soul. Only connection, human connection and a connection to God, will create a feeling of having enough. Everything else is a backward, wrong-way route where we think we're taking care of our needs, while only pulling ourselves farther from them.

Whether we recognize it or not, everything we do can be broken down to the need to belong, fit in, and be accepted by others. We want to connect. But the way we connect to others depends on how we connect with ourselves. If we are disconnected from our own heart, we lack self-love. When we don't have love for ourselves, we don't have love in our hearts, and we have nothing to give to others. This is what creates neediness: We want to get love without giving it up ourselves. A needy soul usually attaches him- or herself to a person in their community who they think will fix or save them. It's an impossible demand, since fixing or saving someone can only happen when you open your heart chakra and love yourself first.

When you learn how to love yourself first, you can become independent from the community and independent from the people on whom your learned to rely, either physically or emotionally. And it is only when you are independent, when you can sustain yourself with self-love, that you can fully connect to others and be a part of a community. So being in a community teaches us both to disconnect from it and to connect with it.

We need to connect with others for a variety of reasons. The most obvious reason we need and depend on each other is for the survival of the human species through the process of procreation. As the saying goes, it takes two to tango, and a community can exist in as small of a number as two.

My earliest memory of learning how other families operate was in sixth grade. There was a girl in my class named Becca. She and I became fast friends when we started working on a school science project together. One day, she invited me to her house so we could make our potato-powered lightbulb for school. It was a big deal to get my mom to give me permission to go anywhere but straight home after school. As I've mentioned, there were so many cousins and friends around the neighborhood to play with that there was no reason to go anywhere else but home. I did go to Girl Scout meetings and activities, but that was different. Because Becca and I were going to work on our project, my mom surprisingly allowed me to go to her house. I guess she was having a good day.

Becca lived adjacent to the schoolyard and walked home all by herself. I rarely walked anywhere by myself. At that age, my sister, Susan, walked me to and from school every day. I knew for sure that my mom would never agree to me walking home without an adult, so I figured I would keep this unsupervised little jaunt a secret. As we approached Becca's house, Becca stopped on the sidewalk and started fishing around in her backpack. She fumbled with all the books and papers and was grumbling under her breath. When I asked her what she was looking for, she said, "My house key." *House key?* I thought. *Why don't I have a house key? Why does she need a house key? Since when does a kid carry a house key? Isn't the door unlocked? And if the door is locked, why wouldn't her mom just let her in the house?* In those couple of minutes I decided that her mother was probably too far away to get to the door to let us in. Or maybe she was in the kitchen cooking some giant, fabulous meal, and she couldn't leave the stove long enough to open the door. I couldn't wait for what I imagined to be the best after-school snack any mother ever created!

When Becca opened the door, there were no wonderful smells coming from the kitchen. There were no noises of someone upstairs or in another room. The house was eerily silent. It all felt very foreign to me. I couldn't think of a time when I'd come home from school and *not* seen my mother. My mother was as sure a sight as the couch in the living room or the refrigerator in the kitchen. She was part of my home. I didn't consciously realize it then, but I can look back now and see that my home and the people in it were what grounded me. Having my mother at home, knowing that my family was always there for me, was what gave me the courage *not to* be there, to leave, to grow up and move out.

I soon learned that Becca's mom and dad had divorced. Her mother, like many mothers and fathers, was working full-time to support Becca and her sister (who had gone home with a friend that day when I went to Becca's). Walking into an empty house was normal for Becca. At first, I felt uncomfortable being there without an adult around. I was a family-based kid, who didn't quite know what to do when not surrounded by cousins, aunts, uncles, my sister, and brothers. After a few minutes, though, it felt cool to be cut loose from my family. Becca and I could make decisions on our own—we didn't need approval. We were liberated! I watched Becca move around the house. She went to the fridge, took out some leftover pizza, and then she did the unthinkable—she turned on the oven! *Wow!* I thought Becca was one of the luckiest girls I knew.

Eventually, as Becca and I grew closer and closer, I saw all the responsibility that had been heaped on her. She felt the full burdens of adulthood as she took care of her sister—feeding her and helping her with homework—most days after school. I started to wonder whether Becca, with all her freedom and independence, really was the lucky one. Was it nice that there wasn't an adult breathing down her neck, telling her to do her homework and to set the table? Or was it awful that she had to make dinner for herself and her sister, and had to breathe down her sister's neck telling her to do homework? The more time I spent with Becca, the more joy I experienced at the sight of my mom preparing a delicious Italian meal for my dad, my brothers, my sister, and me. Having a mother and a home like that, I realized, wasn't guaranteed for anyone. In fact, it wasn't necessarily the norm. Each family, I discovered, did things differently, followed different customs.

Now that I hold the wisdom that has been passed on to me from the spirit world, I understand that Becca's situation was no better or worse than mine. Each one of us is exactly where The Universe wants us to be at a particular time. There were lessons Becca learned from her very small family, where she was as important a leader as her mother. And there were lessons that I learned from my large family, where I was part of the flock helmed by my mother and my grandmother, who lived with us.

Humans operating in their three-dimensional bodies always want what they cannot have. The opposite end of the spectrum appeals to us. But the differences between us, the differences in our communities, gives us varied experiences that teach us the lessons we were meant to learn in family life. Every person we encounter, every meal we eat, every relationship we have within and outside our communities teaches us something new that leads us through the blueprint God devised with us before we entered our bodies.

Becca knew her family and the customs of her family. Those customs made her the wonderful person she is today. And I knew my family and the customs of my family, which made me who I am today. Each of us was acclimated to the specific ways of our community. We both felt comfortable and safe.

Often you don't question the way things are, since you fully trust the leaders of your family (usually parents and grandparents). We believe the things they do, we eat the foods they eat, we read the newspapers and magazines they read. All these habits, while we're under their influence, usually feel like the "right" way, since it is our family's way, and the way of many generations before us.

When I got over being enamored with Becca's freedom, I started feeling sorry for her. Becca always spoke highly of her mother. They were so close that Becca told her everything, even things I'd never have dreamed of telling my mother! Becca never felt alone in her small family—she felt bound to her sister and mother as though they were triplets. Still, I assumed her life was worse than mine because her mother needed to work and wasn't there when Becca got home from school. Boy, was I wrong! Although life was different in her house than it was in mine and my cousins', Becca didn't think that her family's way was any worse. It was her reality; she accepted it and was happy within it and didn't know any other way. We had two very different realities.

Becca may have missed out on the kind of childhood I had, but I missed out on the kind of freedom she had. As time went by, each of us made new friends, and eventually my family moved to a new town. It wasn't until the appearance of social media that I was able to reconnect with Becca. I wasn't shocked to find out how well she did for herself. Today, Becca is a high school nurse. She and her husband own a very successful day camp, which she coruns in the summer. Becca's camp encourages children to explore and create while taking safe risks—just as Becca had done on her own as a kid. Becca's childhood experiences, filled with adult responsibilities, taught her everything she needed to know to be a nurturer and to start her own business of helping children thrive. It seems silly now to think that I had felt bad for her. She was doing great following God's blueprint back then, and she continues to do great today. This is one example that proves that everything we observe in others is only our own perception derived from our particular reality. I'm so happy for Becca's success and proud to call her my friend.

Becca and I may have been from very different families, but we got along great because, at our core, we vibrated on the same frequency. We "got" each other. As we get older, we often don't open ourselves up to new people. We feel as if we don't have time for more people, or time to get to know someone. The problem with this is that we might be settling with the wrong people while letting the right people pass us by.

The Universe knows where you're supposed to go in this life; a plan has been set for you. As I've said before, you can take the easy route or the hard way. That's what free will is: the ability to figure out how to get to the place that's been predetermined for you. Well, I'm here to tell you—whatever route you take, the journey will be much easier if you are surrounded by a community. We all have different gifts and talents we can bring to the table to help each other. While trying to navigate your soul's journey, when you are part of a community, not only can you rely on gifts and talents beyond your own, but you can use the strength and the power of the group for protection and security.

We are all part of The Universal Mind, tapped into the same energy field. Our essential needs are universal, and these needs don't change as we age. When we work in groups we see ourselves from a different angle. In other words, surrounding yourself with people gives you perspective on yourself. No, you are not the center of the universe and the most important person around. And no, you are not the least important person around. You are equal, though what you have to give is different from what others have to give. What you need, your weaknesses, are likely different from others' weaknesses too. When we attach ourselves to communities, these strengths and weaknesses, some of which we didn't even know we had, can be seen in relief against the background of others (again, the **Law of Polarity**).

There is enormous benefit in creating a community from people of many different backgrounds. You know how purebred dogs get recessive birth defects over time? Poodles, with their runny, gunky eyes, are a result of being purebred. When you crossbreed animals, you weed out the recessive genes and create stronger, more adaptable animals. (By the way, I love all dogs, even purebred poodles!) The same is true for our minds and souls. When we bring into our life people who have lived in places we haven't, people who have done things we haven't, who can speak languages we can't speak, the entire group benefits. We don't learn as much from someone with the same beliefs, history, and experiences as ours, as from someone who has lived a life that is foreign to us. And when we stop learning, we stop living. Each time you create a new community from people of variegated backgrounds, you create a whole that is much greater, stronger, and smarter than its parts.

There are many systems and institutions in life where individual variety is introduced to create a better whole. Look at our justice system: A jury of 12 is chosen so that varying points of view, ideas, and opinions can go into deciding the fate of a single individual.

And what about the car you're driving? The community that created it included factory workers in Detroit or Germany or Japan, engineers, mechanics, metal workers, designers, ad executives, voice-over artists—the list goes on. If you take any one category of worker away, you don't end up with a car.

What about a symphony or a rock band? I'll talk about a rock band, since they're smaller. Could the Beatles have succeeded if John, Paul, George, and Ringo were all guitar players? Could the Rolling Stones have succeeded if Mick, Keef (*sic!*), Charlie, and Ronnie all just sang, played no instruments, and pranced around on stage doing moves like Jagger? I mentioned earlier that I like to view communities and friendships as I would good teamwork: efficiently working together, with each member contributing their respective gifts and assets toward the betterment of the whole.

Let's look at a sports team. I'm from New York, so I'll use the Yankees as an example. Not only do they win as a team, they lose as a team. Each team member counts on the other to pull him through, help him out, especially when they are out in the field. If one player drops the ball, another will run to try to pick it up and throw it to base. Besides having each other to lean on, they also have the wisdom and oversight of the team manager. The manager sits outside the game, outside the plays, but watches the whole team. He, above all, understands the interconnectedness, how one player's bad elbow affects another player's need to warm up, and so forth. The way a manager interacts with his team is similar to how our creator interacts with us: Each is part of the whole while guiding and leading the individuals within the whole. Also, both spend a lot of time sitting back and observing the moves of the team and the individuals on it. When he (and He) sees the game slipping, each springs into action to save the day. The players have to trust the manager, just as they have to trust themselves. They learn to listen to his wisdom and run faster with his shouts and pep talks. They are all separate parts of a complete system—just as you and I are individual parts of the singular Universe and the vibrating energy that connects us and makes us a part of one Divine Mind.

As a young woman, I was able to move out of the house, work in Manhattan, and travel freely because I knew I had the support of my family. I still have that wonderful family today, though my community has expanded to include my husband's family, the family my husband and I created together, and members of my spiritual community. I also have my group of besties. We consult with each other on everything and rely on one another for encouragement and strength. We laugh and cry together, all expressions of our great love for each other.

Here I am, a grown working woman, a mother, and a wife, and I will always need the support of friends and family, of many communities!

As kids, we get the family we get through birth or adoption, or foster parents. Unfortunately, there are times when this family of origin feels wrong. Some people look around at the customs and ways of their family of origin and think, *How did I end up here with these people? These people are nothing like me!* This happens more often than you might think. People who are raised in a family that feels foreign to them were usually sent to that family to teach them many different lessons such as compassion, acceptance, forgiveness, or generosity. Sometimes these lessons aren't learned until the family "outsider" has passed on.

There are people in my family who are praying for me every day. I so appreciate their prayers—prayers help us all. But they aren't praying for me in the way you might imagine. In fact, they're praying for me because they think that my psychic gifts pull me away from God as we learned about Him in the Catholic church. These family members believe I have strayed from my religion. I still love these people dearly and I know that one of my purposes is to teach them Christ's love, which is all love and all energy—which is what we feel when we open our heart chakra.

As you likely have already figured out, I have remained faithful to Christianity in my devotion to following the Christ Consciousness. Through my discourse with the spirit world, I have come to learn that there is only one universal religion, and that is *love*—and only one universal race, and that is the human race. To follow Christ Consciousness means to become more like Christ. When Jesus Christ lived on Earth as a man (made of flesh and bone), he did not ask that we follow him, as in follow him the man. Rather he asked that we follow his lead in spirit—how we conduct ourselves in this world—how we live and treat others. His teaching of practicing unconditional love toward others is very much alive to this day, dwells inside each one of us, and is still the main message God wants us to remember.

One thing that my spirit guides can't stress enough is this: When we leave our physical bodies and return to meet our maker, we can't escape going over the life we have just lived on Earth. During this life review, one question will come up that is of the utmost importance: How much did you love?

When you are with the right team, feeling and giving love feels easy.

If you find yourself the odd one out in a wrong-feeling family, you should not close your heart to the love and comfort of this family. In fact, you should do the opposite. Understand that your role here was to show the family something they otherwise would not understand. Or perhaps you needed to be born into that family to learn individuality: Since you rarely agree with your family's mindset, you were probably called a rebel. That is okay. Don't accept that negative label; instead, think of yourself as unique and different, as most innovators are. Then peacefully walk away with an open and loving heart and you will soon find a new group or community who understands and accepts you and all of your quirky ways—a community who vibrates at the same level as you. Whatever you do, do not isolate yourself from others. Perhaps you need to do this for a short time in order to regroup or clear your head, but I don't recommend going solo long term.

But how do we find new people for our chosen adult families? How do successful rock bands come together? Why are some baseball teams working together in a perfect groove while others seem to be faltering? The answer—for me, you, the Yankees, and rock bands—is this: The people in communities pick each other, whether we're aware of it or not. Remember, *your vibe attracts your community*. It's part of the **Law of Attraction:** like is attracted to like. What you might not understand is that, as an adult fending for yourself in the world, the people who are like you aren't necessarily the people who grew up in a similar community with similar parents or religious training. This is especially true if you were the "outcast" in your family of origin, the person sent to teach them tolerance, among other things.

The people you feel an immediate connection with, the people you feel most comfortable with, are those who have similar vibrational frequencies. They are the people who "get you." Remember, these people are searching for you as hard as you are searching for them (consciously or subconsciously). To some degree they have similar interests and goals. They think in ways that complement the ways you think, and their language is on the same wavelength, energetically. Finding your community, or allowing the people of your community to find you, can be a very rewarding endeavor. You might start off with different idiomatic expressions and cute little sayings, but when you sync your vibe with someone, eventually you'll be sharing your silly slang too.

Years ago, I taught a class on developing psychic abilities. This class took place in a karate studio, so the students started calling me Sensei. In that class were 20 very different people of varying ages, races, and economic standing. But they had two things in common: a desire to learn how to cultivate their God-given gifts, and the desire to share these gifts with the world. Although I taught this particular group of students almost 10 years ago, I am very proud to say that my students are all still connected at the hip (metaphorically) and are helping each other grow and thrive. All of them have fulfilled their goals and have realized their dream: to use their abundant gifts to help the world. The bonds formed in this class are so strong and connected that they will transcend this life and will continue to bind them on the other side. Profound connections do that—they transcend all dimensions.

Being nestled in a community gives you the courage Disney spoke of to pursue your dreams. When you have a safe place to land, jutting out into the universe doesn't feel so scary. You will know when you've landed with the right people because everything will feel easy. You'll feel like yourself and not a false self you may have created to get along with your family of origin. Being with the right people feels as natural as breathing. It takes no effort or work to be with the right community. It is a way of being with God, a way of feeling the power of love.

There are also communities within the spirit world. I have talked to spirits who were part of my community on the other side. We made a pact with God to help each other out in the three-dimensional world. (I think many people in the class where I was called Sensei had made pacts with each other on the other side.) So many of the people who have come to me and helped shape my life were acting on the blueprint created with God and my spirit guides. They were following through on an agreement made together in the spirit world. These souls were always going to enter this life I'm in now to help direct me to my soul purpose.

The child who dies in a drunk-driving accident may have agreed to that end with his spirit guides and God. It was part of the blueprint, the master plan. His purpose may have been to lead his parents to their soul purpose, which might be to teach others about safe driving and sober driving. They might be on this three-dimensional Earth to show people the ways in which personal responsibility is really responsibility toward the group, toward mankind, toward the biggest team of them all.

Routes to our soul purpose might not come in such dramatic ways. The magician who showed up at your eighth birthday party, who sparked your interest in magic, which led you to the magic shop where you met your husband (the greatest love of your life) may have showed up at your party because of an agreement you and he made on the other side. His agreement with you led you to the place where you could learn about love, commitment, and family.

And it can be through collaboration with others, finding a community with which you vibe, that you may discover your soul purpose. This is how I discovered my soul purpose:

I am a big believer in the saying *Give a man a fish, he'll eat for a day; teach a man to fish, he'll eat for a lifetime.* The teaching part of that statement fits right into who I am today. But you should know that not so many years ago, I had no idea that I had the ability, the gift, to teach. When I joined the psychic community, I learned so much from so many people who had been doing this longer than I. I also learned things about myself: One of those things is that any information that goes in me starts kicking and fighting to come back out of me in the form of a lesson. In other words, I'm a natural teacher who thrives on helping people.

When I meet a person, I don't notice much about their external appearance. Instead, through my gift of interpreting energy, I look directly into their heart and their soul. This allows me to see who they really are. It also allows me to see their strengths and weaknesses, even ones they don't know they have. When I get the chance, I enjoy sharing with people my accumulated knowledge of them, so I can help them see the beauty inside themselves.

I consider myself a cheerleader for other people's souls. I am deeply humbled through my teachings and take great pride in the many people who have discovered their unique gifts through me. Each person

I teach teaches others and helps others. This chain of learning and teaching, learning and teaching, creates a ripple effect that spreads throughout the world. It was only through collaboration with others, through my community connections, that I discovered my soul purpose: to teach, serve, empower, and love.

When you surround yourself with a group of individuals, a team, where all the parts are working for the greater good of the whole, miracles will happen all around you. This is the highest, purest, most Godlike way to live. It is what we should aspire to. I am connected to you. You are connected to me. And we, together, are connected to God. So let's work as one, for all the beautiful miracles, for the greater good of all. For the human family!

SOUL KIT

Finding Your Team

When my spirit guides instructed me to teach my first psychic development class, I was very obliging, but I wondered where I would get the students with the proper credentials to be in my class. I had no idea that there was an internet group called Meetup. When I asked my spirit guides where I would get the students for my class, I coincidentally came across this website. Of course, we all know that there is no such thing as coincidence. What I later found out was that only one student who came from the Meetup internet site was meant to be in my class, though at least eight people from that advertisement came and interviewed with me. The student from the Meetup group has flourished like a beautiful flower and she is now my good friend and an amazing reader of the Akashic Records.

What I also learned was, just by having blind faith and agreeing to teach this class at the directive of my spirit guides, they were the very same beings that took control in helping me connect the rest of the dots. Before I knew it, my clients were all asking me how they could further develop their psychic gifts. Word of mouth spread, and before long I had enough people to teach many classes.

My advice to you, then, is to take that first step: Take a leap of faith to find the right team for you and decide what type of group you would like to participate in. Use your gifts and talents to teach others what you've learned—or become the student and join a class of like-minded individuals who share similar interests and passions. Here is what I recommend: Make a list of your five favorite activities. Number them in order, with 1 as your most favorite.

1. Next to each activity, write a list of the places where other people do this activity. It doesn't matter if it's a solitary activity like reading or watching TV; there are places where those things are still done.

2. Get on the internet and Google groups that regularly engage in that activity, even if it's something done alone, like reading. There are always several different Meetup groups or other types of groups on the internet consisting of people who have the same interests as you. Write down the groups next to each of the five activities.

3. Make a list of other people you know who you think may enjoy the same activities. Write down their names next to each item on your list.

4. Devote one month to trying out a group for each activity. If it's something like reading, you might go to a book club. If it's something like gardening, you might join a horticulture society. Side note: One of my sons

recently relocated to a new state and he loves to bowl, so he decided to join a bowling league. He has made friends who share his interest. I am so happy he feels more like he belongs in his new surroundings.

My guess is: If you give five different activities a one-month trial, you will end up finding at least one community where you feel like a vital, integral, and connected part of the whole.

7

Surrender!
Let Go of Control and Let Your Soul Take the Lead

> *"Sometimes surrender means giving up trying to understand and becoming comfortable with not knowing."*
> —ECKHART TOLLE

WHEN I was a kid, my mother often reminded me, "I brought you into this world and if necessary, I can take you out!" This is a pretty harsh statement coming from one of the most important people in my life. She was the person I had my very first connection with as I journeyed into my current physical body as Kim. Even at a fairly young age, I liked to think about the fact that my mother cradled me inside her for nine months. This thought, that she protected me, and then brought me out to breathe air when I was ready, gave me a warm, fuzzy feeling. But to insinuate that she had the wherewithal to take me out of this world when I misbehaved? That did not sit well with me. Not at all! Was my own mother planning on committing murder if I didn't do my homework and clean my room? Of course, she wasn't. And, of course, I never really feared for my life. If there was one thing that was certain in my household, it was that you'd be fed and you'd be loved. Still, even in that happy home, threats like this were thrown around like undercooked spaghetti at the wall. Few, if any, ever stuck.

Many of you have probably heard this very same threat, or a version of it, from one of your parents. And chances are, your parents learned the phrase from their parents, and so on. I have to admit, I've uttered these same words to my boys a couple of times. Of course, I know better, but it just slipped out of me. Words like these are used as a fear tactic, plain and simple. There are many versions of this threat, created to scare an innocent child into doing what we've asked. It's a form of desperation on the adult's part (authority figure)—a frantic reach for control.

Often, we identify control with power. And many of us feel that if we don't micromanage every detail of our lives (and our children's or partner's lives too) that we are slacking in our roles as mother/father/wife/husband/child, etc. We feel powerless. Additionally, we falsely equate being a good human being with being able to control everything around us.

Negative programming is abundant in people trying to exert control. And issues of control—the need, desire, urge, and act of controlling—all come out of fear—and all of this, as we already know, is born out of the ego. Our first experience of fear usually happens within our family of origin. We are taught what to fear, how to fear, when to fear, and whom to fear. Of course, you need to fear a mountain lion if it's charging toward you. But other than actual physical threats, fear is not part of the divine plan, and does not serve you. I know I spoke about the emotion of *fear* in a previous chapter, but I bring it up here again to point out how fear creeps into our lives in so many different ways. It paralyzes us and keeps us stuck in the perpetual loop of restricted beliefs, preventing us from growing or moving forward. Fear is what we learn in the three-dimensional life; it is the opposite of what our divine spirits are made of, which is love. Fear is crippling, while love is liberating. Anything that is not made of love is not part of your divine plan.

Fear leads to the need to control. Among other things, we fear that things won't turn out as we want them to. When we feel the need to control, it is because we are attached to yielding a particular, desired outcome. The wise and loving Buddha put it perfectly when he said, "The root of suffering is attachment." We can have attachments to people, places, and things, as well as to opinions, ideas, and beliefs. When we are rooted in our attachments, we are certain to bring great disappointment and anxiety into our lives. Our attachment to things is an attempt to fill the voids in our hearts with material items. It doesn't take long after acquiring a thing to realize that the "fix" was only temporary. The void persists, so we search for even more items: bigger, better, more expensive. When we attach to relationships—when we try to control them to have a particular, desired outcome—we end up feeling disappointed, rejected, anxious, or even angry. The expectations we have for other people can easily flip into anger that sets up shop in our hearts, blocking all the radiating light of our heart chakra.

Disappointment rarely has to do with the person we're disappointed with; rather, it gives us information about ourselves. If you respond to disappointment by looking inward, you will often be able to see which part of you appears broken, wounded, or needy. What's likely is that we project and attach ourselves to results we want from the other person; we expect them to heal us or fix something broken inside us. The answer to disappointment is not to "right" the person you're disappointed with, but to fix inside yourself the thing you projected onto them. When we heal our own hearts, we can see clearly how our disappointments have nothing to do with other people.

Often the qualities that attracted us to another person are the strong characteristics that we ourselves are lacking. We hope that we can acquire these qualities from these people, or that in attaching ourselves to these people, their qualities become ours too. We may do this consciously or unconsciously. Conversely, the other person may have been attracted to parts of you that they felt could heal them. These relationships can work, and people can learn from each other and adopt each other's habits. Sometimes, though, if this is the entire basis of the relationship, people will move on after the lessons have been learned. The person who is left behind often feels lost, with no idea how to pick up the pieces to reassemble the life they want, the relationship they want, and the relationship they need to have with themselves.

At various times in our lives, we will either play the role of the teacher or the student; sometimes we play both roles at once. If you fail to recognize the root of your need and suffering, you might spend a lifetime trying to learn the same lesson over and over with the same person, or by cycling through different people. Look at a lineup of past relationships. How many times were the lessons and outcome the same, even though you moved on to a different person?

Your soul remembers all the lives it's lived through. It knows what it needs to learn and overcome in each lifetime. Your soul is far more in sync with the vibrations of The Universe than it is with your three-dimensional body. The ego and the analytical mind are connected to the three-dimensional body. They get in the way of what the soul knows and can direct you away from what you really need or away from the lessons you need to learn. Our ego leads us to believe that we can control the world around us and can create the "perfect" outcome for any given situation. But, as I've said many times before, "Life doesn't work out on paper." In other words, life cannot be lived through logic alone. In fact, the opposite is true.

This is the great beauty of our journey in these three-dimensional bodies: We have the free will to choose and to create a dream life. The Universe will support our desires and decisions *as long as our desires and decisions support the plan of the soul.* I love this quote from Paulo Coelho's book *The Alchemist*: ". . . and when you want something, all the universe conspires in helping you to achieve it." This is true. If you step back and let The Universe do its work, you'll see it in action.

When you try to control an outcome of any given situation, it puts a great deal of pressure on any individual (including yourself) to "deliver the goods." It's good to have goals and visions of what you want to see come to fruition in your life. But it is impossible to come up with a play-by-play plan for how you will enact this vision. (Remember the adage "Man plans, and God laughs.") What if the vision you have for your life is less than what The Universe, in all its divine wisdom, has for you? What if The Universe's plan for you is bigger and better than you could have ever imagined? Do not put limits on God—God is limitless.

A person who is afraid to fail and a person who won't stop until they succeed are different versions of a human believing their own story. I pray that if you believe your own story, and if it's not a good one, you will surrender to a different story. Surrender to God's B plan for you. (When you learn to surrender control, your secondary and tertiary plans—God's plans—often become your A plans.) In order to follow these new plans, you have to let go and detach from the plans you thought you had to follow. You have to surrender!

The word *surrender* means to stop resisting energy that is pushing back. When we're in control mode, it almost feels as if we are fighting against an invisible force. To surrender is to let go and stop fighting. When we surrender and lean back into the flow of The Universe, with all its divine wisdom, suddenly all the answers to the questions we're asking just appear.

The answers might be a little hard to read. Sometimes they may look like an instruction sheet from IKEA, which comes with an Allen wrench and a whole pile of nuts, bolts, and screws of varying size. You know that if you can put the nuts and bolts in the right place, if you insert Tab A into Tab B at the right angle, you'll have created something solid. But if you ignore some of the bolts, skimp on the directions, throw away the wrench, and try to use a screwdriver instead, you might end up with something a little wobbly and off-kilter—just as life seems to be at times. (If you've ever purchased a piece of furniture from IKEA, you know what I'm talking about.)

God, or The Universe, is omnipresent, omniscient, and omnipotent. This means that God is everywhere, knows everything, and is all-powerful. This Intelligence has the power to know everything about the past, the present, and the future. Remember, time is not linear in the spirit world. This is a hard concept to grasp, though Einstein got it. (God's mind is even greater than Einstein's, of course.) God has ways to solve problems that you would never be able to conjure up, not in a million years. The Universe has the wherewithal to connect the dots in your life perfectly without missing a single freckle. As it is with any child who instinctively trusts his parents to nurture, care, love, and protect him, so too should we, as the children of The Universe, put our trust and faith in our heavenly parent.

The Universe is designed to help you manifest your greatest dreams and desires. And it does this in magical and effortless ways. Because our vision is restricted in our three-dimensional bodies, we can never see the immeasurable ways in which everything in the universe is so intrinsically linked. But when you rise above your limited point of view, when you allow The Spirit to lead, you can discover that the possibilities are vast and endless, beyond what you ever imagined. I believe that this all-seeing spiritual point of view is where the term *mastermind* comes from.

When we learn to quiet our monkey mind and focus on quieting the voice of that pesky ego that continually feeds us the lie that we're in control—that is when we truly master the mind and embrace the truth. In other words, when we stop thinking, the mastermind can take over and think for us.

When I look back on my life, I can see there are many times when I thought I had control over my life, but clearly didn't. It was only when I learned the art of surrendering (and I must give credit to my spirit peeps for teaching me this) that I was able to enjoy a life free of anxiety. (Well, most of the time.) I've always loved surprises, but now I love them even more, since I see that they are the twists and turns The Universe has planned for me. Just when I think things are going one way, God puts a different spin on things. I know how to see the signs, and I understand that I should follow God's trail rather than insisting on sticking to my original plan.

Now you might be asking why we're all such control freaks. The answer is simple: You may have grown up listening to people in your family argue, or overhearing phone conversations between your mother and your aunt where they deconstructed every family member down to his or her core faults. It is even probable that, as a young child, you knew how to solve the problems plaguing your family. If you were like me, you assumed your elders knew better, so you didn't speak up. Some of you may have spoken up, but you were told you were too young to understand, or that *children are to be seen and not heard*. Either way, in most cases *your voice was not heard*.

When a child's voice is not heard, they can feel powerless. That feeling carries into adulthood. As we grow up, we grasp onto everything around us, trying to have our voices heard, wanting to take control of a life that felt out of our control when we were young. Is this starting to sound familiar to you?

No one forgets the difficulties they experienced or witnessed as a kid, and everyone wants to create an adulthood that doesn't include any of the same problems. We claim we will never become involved with someone who acts in the ways our troubled or troubling family members acted. We vow never to live in the compromised circumstances we lived in as kids. This desire makes us control freaks of a sort. We want to drive the bus so that it goes exactly where we want it to go. The problem is that only God can really take the wheel, and that bus will only go where He wants it to go. It's hard to surrender when you have the forceful memory of your childhood stirring inside you.

Meanwhile, despite our best efforts, many of us still carry and recapitulate one or more bad habits from our childhood families. Some people, even those trying to exert the most control, fully mimic the actions of their original family and implement all the unhealthy behaviors, along with the healthy ones, in their adult communities and families. Many of us put off learning truths about ourselves and our behaviors until we've put decades behind us of unhealthy patterns and actions. And we all know many people, if not ourselves, who have behaved in healthy ways for years and then fell into old, destructive patterns and behaviors. We are always changing and evolving. Sometimes, we're devolving too. But I've got good news for you: You are never too old to learn to let go of these habits, give up control, and surrender the illusion of being in control. Yes, control is only an illusion.

Many of you reading this book may be going through the toughest part of your life journey. Others may be in a process of healing from what is known as *"the dark night of the soul."* No matter where you are in your life at this moment, you understand what it's like to be at a low point. As a psychic medium, I have been fortunate in that I get to speak to wise souls who have completed their Earthly lives and have ascended into the nonphysical realm. I call these souls wise, because what they can see from where they are now is so much greater than what we see from our three-dimensional bodies. We've all heard the expression *Hindsight is 20/20.* And we all know it to be true. There's also the saying *If I knew then what I know now . . .* Yes, spirits have hindsight.

As humans, we tend to believe in only what's tangible—things that we can see and touch. In order to find something to be "true," we want it to make sense within the system of beliefs we've learned in the three-dimensional world, the beliefs we learned from our families and in the other communities we've developed. Most, but not all, of these beliefs—our own and those passed down to us—stem from the very restricted and limited view from a three-dimensional body. And many of these beliefs have an origin in fear. Think of the family where each generation follows the next into the family business because, "that's what we do." There are definitely people in that family who are afraid to follow their gut (their heart, their soul!) and do something that isn't part of the family business.

I know a guy, let's call him Matthew, who wanted to be an EMT instead of running the family hardware store. Matthew never had the faith in his abilities to leave the business. He thought it was in his genes to do what his father, grandfather, and great-grandfather did. I don't know whether running the family business is part of the blueprint plan Matthew made with God—where he's supposed to be—or if it's a detour he created out of the fear of doing anything different from his family. Who knows? Maybe he'll read this book, realize his soul purpose is to save people, and hand over the hardware store to his sister, who is rarely seen without a hammer in her hand and whose soul purpose *does* appear to be working in hardware. One thing I know for sure: Matthew is looking at his situation from a very limited perspective. It's like being in the middle of a bull's-eye (his family business) and trying to see the bull's-eye. You just can't.

Many of the departed souls who have channeled through me express regret over how they limited their journey to the end of their life. They tell me that when they were in their three-dimensional body, they failed to understand the bigger picture. They got caught up in singular focus and minutia, placing undue value, emphasis, and emotional energy on things that barely mattered. And they had issues of control and attachment that kept them from receiving all the gifts and experiences that life had to offer. Think of Matthew, who doesn't believe he can do anything but run his family business: He is unable to detach from that idea.

Once they pass into the spirit world, souls don't have to look at life through the marble-sized lenses of the human eye. Spirits can see the whole picture, the greater meaning. They can look back and witness how wrong their perceptions were and how those misperceptions led them to actions they might not have taken otherwise. So many events in their lives unfolded through the sliver-thin point of view of their three-dimensional bodies. When they were in the same dimension as you and I, they didn't understand or even imagine the interconnectedness of events—events that they can fully understand now that they're being viewed from the multidimensional perspective of a spirit.

During one very eventful reading session, my client, I'll call her Suzie, asked me why she hadn't recognized that her husband had been cheating on her for years. She went on to explain that now, when she looks back, she can see so many signs to which she had been completely blind. She was angry at herself for not having paid better attention and for not having taken the necessary steps to protect her heart, along with her most prized possessions, her children.

The answer to Suzie's question wasn't coming easily to me. Surely, I thought, she must have sensed that something was off with her marriage. And since my guides can hear my thoughts, one of them quickly reminded me that just because signs are put in front of us, doesn't mean people pay attention to them. Not everyone uses their God-given gift of intuition. My spirit guide went on to say that Suzie had never been praised by her family when she was growing up. They continually compared her to her older brother, making her feel invisible. As much as Suzie tried to get her family to notice her by winning numerous awards in high school, along with many other accomplishments, her achievements garnered as much attention as yesterday's news.

Now, as an adult, Suzie's main focus was to gain recognition from others. She was desperate to feel love and acceptance. She did this by trying to control her surroundings—making sure her husband's meals were perfectly cooked when he got home, that his work shirts were picked up from the dry cleaner, and that her children received the best love and attention, certainly better than her mom had given her. Always looking for validation, she found time to volunteer for bake sales at her children's school, and without skipping a beat, made sure to help any one of her friends who was down and out. Suzie was striving to be the best wife, mom, and friend on the planet—reminiscent of Donna Reed, who played the perfect middle-class housewife in the 1960s sitcom *The Donna Reed Show* and the mom in the classic 1946 movie *It's a Wonderful Life*.

My guides continued to answer my question by displaying what seemed to be a feature film onto the blank screen in my mind, connected to my third eye chakra. As I watched the movie, I immediately understood the answer. The reason why Suzie couldn't see her husband's infidelities is the same reason why most of us can't see the big picture of our lives: We have limited perspective.

The guides explained that the difference in perspective between the three-dimensional body and a spirit is like the difference between looking out an airplane window while on the ground and looking out an airplane window while in the sky. When you're sitting on the ground you can see other planes out the window, and the open carts with baggage and the guys wearing jumpsuits and headphones, waving those lighted wands. The terminal where you'd been waiting a while ago is also visible. It's a lot to see, but it's all contained within that particular terminal at the airport. That's what it's like to "see" when you're alive in your three-dimensional body.

When that plane takes off, however, you see more like what the spirits see. Within seconds, you can see the whole airport. A little higher and you see the whole city. Isn't it amazing how many baseball fields there are? Higher still, and you marvel at how the roadways all cross each other and are intertwined and connected. This is something that's impossible to see when you're driving those very same roads. From way up there, the houses line up in perfect rows—they look like the houses lined up in *Monopoly.* Higher still, and the lay of the land—mountains and streams, oceans and islands—all becomes clear to us. It's a much broader view that makes that giant airport seem small and insignificant, a bit player in a much bigger show. This is like our lives: The show is much bigger than just us.

If only my friend Matthew could float up into space and see himself standing in that hardware store—he would see his sister managing everything, his mother happily making dinner in the house in back of the hardware store, his dad relaxing, reading the newspaper now that he's retired. Matthew might also see the EMT training school a half hour away in another town. He might see that it would be easy to commute there while also helping out his sister at the store every now and then. He would see that leaving the family business wouldn't mean leaving the family. Leaving the family business might make Matthew a more valued member of his community. Maybe, if he became an EMT, he'd save the life of someone in his family one day.

And if Suzie hadn't tried to be the perfect wife, the perfect mom, and the perfect friend—if she had instead invited the intelligence of The Universe to help her—she would have been given a broader point of view. In loving herself more and managing her time differently, she would not have been so exhausted. Exhaustion is a way of staying in a low vibration and keeps you close to the Earth; it prevents you from having a bird's-eye view. Suzie needed to love herself more and surrender to her imperfections. She needed to learn that she is perfect just as she is, equal to God and all of his love. Who is to say that Suzie's husband wouldn't have done what he did if she were paying closer attention, however, had she let go of her fears and surrendered to love sooner, she would have been more grounded, calm, and focused, thereby affording her the opportunity to see the truth—the truth of the whole situation, and the truth would have set her free.

When spirits leave their physical bodies, it's like taking off on an airplane. They can look down and see the whole map of their lives, every twist and turn, and how it's connected to the twists and turns of other lives—people they knew and people they didn't know. The ways in which each life event unfolded is crystal clear to the spirit. Besides having a clearer picture and an aerial view of the life they just led, the spirit world understands how The Universe works.

The spirits—my personal spirit guides, angels, and ascended masters with whom I've spoken—have all imparted valuable wisdom that has changed the way I live in my three-dimensional body. Even though the limitations of my physical body prevent me from physically seeing past this body, I can visualize and understand the wider point of view. I can see things in the ways the spirits see them. Part of my soul purpose is to share this wisdom with you in the hope that it will resonate as true and touch your soul on as deep a level as it has touched mine.

I pray for all my readers to let go of the limited thoughts that keep them from living a stress-free, wonderful life. Just as I want Matthew and Suzie to understand the alternate ways they could navigate through their soul's blueprint, I want you, too, to allow The Universe to do its job in helping you on your journey.

Here's another scenario to show you how attachment to the vision from the three-dimensional body can limit you. My friend Anya, who lives in Northern California, told me a story about planning a special day for her boyfriend, Johnny. She consulted her friend Dan, who told her about a magical hike near a stream in the Oakland hills. Dan said his day spent near trees and water, walking on a narrow dirt path, gave him a bird's-eye view of his own life and all he had to be grateful for.

Anya left work three hours early to buy a backpack and food for this day trip. She wanted everything to be perfect for Johnny, and she wanted a bird's-eye view of her life too.

You can probably guess how this story goes, since you've certainly experienced something like this at some point in your life. Yes, it rained that day and their hike was a muddy trek. Yes, they couldn't go near the stream, since it was rushing with treacherous brown water. And yes, Anya locked the keys in the car and they had to wait two hours in the rain (with no umbrella, of course, but lots of wet food) for AAA to show up.

When Anya called Dan the next day to complain about her disastrous date, when she did *not* get a bird's-eye view of her life, Dan said, "Guess what? It's all good, God is going to give you another day, without rain, and you can take that hike again—or even a different hike. How great is that?!"

Let's look at what happened in the story above. Three people went to the same place but came home with totally different experiences. Anya and Johnny, after extensive preparations, had a terrible day. In trying to recreate the wonderful experience Dan had, Anya was attached to a preconceived outcome—and had expectations of how things *should* have been. Anya was looking at this single day from the limited point of view of her three-dimensional body: in that very small space and at that very small sliver of time. When the day proved to be out of her control—when God had a different plan—she deemed it a disaster.

Dan, on the other hand, thought it was such a great experience he almost couldn't find the words to describe it. He had no attachment to how his journey up the mountain went. He understood his lack of control and accepted what The Universe handed him that day. Dan was able to live in the moment, *surrendering* to the beauty of The Universe that was all around him.

Remember in *The Wizard of Oz* when the wicked witch, flying in the air with her broomstick, writes with the smoke, *Surrender, Dorothy!* The witch wanted Dorothy to surrender her power (represented by the ruby red shoes) by giving it to her. Dorothy surrendered for a brief time, until she realized the witch had no power over her at all; she only gave the illusion of having power, just like the ego will have you believe. (Note: The wizard and the witch are both symbolic of our ego.) This is no different than the school bully. He gives the illusion of power, but when others push back, he kowtows and walks away with his tail between his legs. This is exactly how our ego mind tries to control us. It comes at us, telling us continuous lies and paralyzes us with fear. But beware, fear can hide itself behind many false identities. It can show up as the powerful authority, or bully (trying to control others), or it can show up as the scared little lost girl like Dorothy trying to find her way home (surrendering her power to others). Ultimately, both of these faces are born from the same emotion of fear, and no matter which mask it hides behind, it will always leave us weak, and powerless.

It wasn't until Dorothy woke up from her nightmare (symbolic for dropping the ego) that she was able to take back her power by opening up her heart (embracing love). Dorothy can finally see the aerial view as she surrenders to the power that was within her all along. This is the power that led her back home (symbolic of The God Force), with a feeling of safety and comfort, and with people who truly love her.

Anya and Johnny were like Dorothy when she surrendered to the witch in surrendering to fear—fear of not having the best date, fear of heights, fear of carrying too much weight, fear of rain, etc. Fear is the witch flying over all of us. Fear comes out of the idea that things should be able to be controlled. I can't stress this enough: Fear and the need to control come out of attachment to projected outcomes.

But you have no control over anything; you cannot determine the outcome of anything. Remember: "Man plans, and God laughs." It's a good saying because it simplifies the ideas of surrender and attachment in a way we all understand.

Fear limits our point of view and our vision. It paralyzes us.

Love opens us up to a larger perspective and liberates us.

Fear restricts us.

Love releases us.

Fear traps us under the spell of the witch.

Love connects us to beauty, magnificence, and God.

When you surrender to love, you become one with The Universe; this is what true freedom is.

Soul Search

FINDING TRUE FREEDOM THROUGH THE COURAGEOUS ACT OF SURRENDERING

1. Do you often see yourself as the victim and blame others for your unfortunate circumstances?

2. Do you ever say, *If only [blank] would happen, then [blank] would happen?*

3. Are you impatient and expect immediate results for your desired outcome?

4. Do you believe your way of doing things is the only correct way?

5. Do you judge others who don't share your opinions or values?

6. Do you believe it's a dog-eat-dog world and the only way to survive is by outsmarting others?

7. Do you make decisions or change plans according to fear?

If you answered yes to any of the questions above, you need to practice detachment and surrender.

When you cast yourself in the role of the victim, you are surrendering to fear and not to God. When you think all good things are conditional on other things, you are ignoring the powers of The Universe.

When you are impatient for results, you are stuck in the simple linear time of the three-dimensional body. When you believe that you are more right than God and The Universe, you are deceiving yourself into thinking you have control. When you judge others who don't share your opinions and values, or think you have to outsmart others to get ahead, you are disregarding the fact that we are all connected through The God Force—we are all one and the same. And when you make decisions from fear-based thinking, you are turning away from love and God.

To act out of fear is to pull yourself away from The Divine. You already know that fear is the opposite of love, but I'll say it again! Each time you are afraid, turn the situation around and find the love. True freedom can only be achieved by letting go of your outdated, programmed belief system. I pray you open your mind, heart, and soul to alternative paths that will lead to your predetermined end. I pray you aren't waiting to become a disembodied spirit in order to live out your soul purpose. You can start living your best life, with passion and purpose, right here, right now, on Earth. I have, and if I can do it, so can you. Let go and surrender to the plan of your soul. Allow the energy of The Universe to be your best collaborator. It knows you inside and out; it remembers why you came here. And, just like the navigation system Waze, it knows the most efficient and quickest route to get your soul to its final destination.

SOUL KIT

Surrender Prayer
Each time you have difficulty surrendering to The Universe, repeat this prayer:

Thank you, Universe, for all that you see and understand. I surrender to your infinite wisdom and endless possibilities in helping me achieve my soul purpose. Please assist me in opening up my heart and allowing the emotion of love to flow through me. This will help me to eliminate all my fear-based thoughts and replace them with loving and safe thoughts. Allow me to view the world with spiritual eyes rather than human eyes, which I know will only limit and restrict my path. Please provide me with strength, grace, and patience.

I surrender any attachments and expected outcomes and humbly surrender to the unseen energy that will allow me to receive the best possible outcome for all concerned. I surrender to your will and I am open to any and all signs you are willing to provide to light the way and pave the road, which will ultimately lead my soul to its highest purpose. I understand that time is an illusion, and what may seem like a lifetime on the Earthly plane may be the blink of an eye in the world in which my soul originated. I am grateful for this opportunity to grow and learn, and I am willing to have blind faith until the end. I thank you for granting me the favor of grace as I struggle to remember the plan of my soul. I humbly thank you in advance.

And so it is, Amen!

Say this every day until you understand your limited vision, have detached from the outcome, and have surrendered to The Higher Power. To do anything else is to remain stuck like Dorothy on that yellow brick road, continually searching in terror for the great and powerful Oz.

8

Everything Is Shaping Up Perfectly: Remembering Your Purpose Through Sacred Patterns of The Universe

> *"It is wisdom to know others;*
> *it is enlightenment to know one's self."*
> —LAO TZU

IN THIS chapter you will learn about all the systems, orders, and patterns in The Universe that show us how we are intricately connected to and part of The God Force. You will see The Divine Hand everywhere—a stamp that marks His presence all around us.

By now, I hope you know that nothing, and I mean nothing in your life, is a coincidence. I explained in my book *The Happy Medium* that we, as souls, map out the life we came here to live before we entered planet Earth.

Our souls are continually evolving. We enter each lifetime to overcome the challenges we faced in past lives, many that have been repeated in more than one incarnation. My spirit guides have told me that coming to planet Earth is like going to a very difficult school for your soul—you have to work really hard to graduate! When I imagine condensing a person's soul into a single human body, I see it as an image of shoving a 100-pound bag of flour into a 25-pound container. The spirit of a man is far more vast than our bodies. It's wonderfully whole and truly without limits. The moment we enter our tiny newborn-baby bodies, we are confined with limited vision and limited choices. There is much that we have to discover, but innately, deep inside each of us, we know that our main goal is to recognize Divine Energy in everything. As we evolve in each life, we awaken to the reality that we are not separate from this energy. Instead, *we are this energy.* When our soul evolves, we learn not to judge others and to forgive them when they fail. In other words, we learn to love unconditionally, as The Higher Power loves us.

Prior to entering a physical form, your soul meets with spirit guides and a council of wise elders, all of this overseen by God, who is everywhere. Together, you carefully choose every aspect of your Earthly life, including where exactly the planets will be in the sky, and what time, down to the second, you will emerge from you mother's womb. Each planetary shift changes who you'll be and how you'll carry yourself in this life. These choices that you make ahead of your birth have very specific intentions. Your parents, too, are chosen (and if you were adopted, you chose that experience as well as your adoptive parents). Although your parents search through numerous lists containing trending baby names prior to your birth, it was really you who picked your name first.

Once you've identified your parents, your soul energy influences your parents to pick your name. After you've been named, you seek meaning and purpose. Above all else, each soul wants to experience happiness and joy every moment possible while still meeting the challenges we need to overcome in order to evolve.

Some souls wish to learn forgiveness and patience. Others might want to learn how to implement more trust. As I've mentioned before, The Universe is all-knowing and wise. This cosmic computer (made up of God, your spirit guides, angels, the cosmic elders, and your soul) puts you with the right people, at the right time, in the right place to make it possible for you to accomplish your soul tasks.

The specific guides who help us create these plans for our lives sit back, waiting and watching from the wings. They cheer us on every step of the way from birth to the final exit. Every now and then, they whisper in our ears and gently remind us of our soul's contract. (If you listen closely, if you tune in, you will know when they are speaking to you.) The guides also help to create synchronistic events that play out during our lives. These events trigger certain emotions that help us make decisions that will aid us in mastering our desired goals.

Now, you're probably wondering why, if we choose all of this—our parents, names, lessons, birthdays—we don't choose the things we're currently wishing for. This is because the soul is full of the wisdom of The Universe—it knows better than to give you a "perfect" life. What could you learn if all was "perfect"? We must always have something important to strive for in order to help motivate us to forge ahead.

Here's how it works. After our chosen soul plan is in place, we enter our mother's womb. Once we're ensconced in the safety of her body, we forget the plan and who we truly are. In the words of the late, great Dolores Cannon, a famous hypnotist and regressionist, "It wouldn't be a test if we knew all of the answers." When we are born, the veil of forgetfulness remains over us so that we may use our free will to work our way toward evolution. Even though there is a plan for us, a goal, and a predetermined exit date (many people may have more than one possible exit time and might bypass the first couple of them), free will gives us the ability to create any reality we choose.

In other words, we can alter the environment in which we navigate our predetermined plan. Still, what people may not realize is that many times when we think we are exercising free will and making choices, we're actually listening to the directives given to us by our Higher Self, our soul, and the spirit guides overseeing us. Much of our subconscious mind is actually our internal connection to those watching over us.

One example of this is who we couple with. Many of our soul mates were not coincidence, or serendipity. Instead, soul mates are brought together by the influences of our souls. The night I met my husband Anthony at a night club is an example of this. I had no intention of partying that evening, but one of my girlfriends would not let up! She pushed and pushed until I agreed to go to a club with her. Looking back on it now, I can see that my spirit guides were influencing her to get me to go out. The guides have the power to do that; they will work through everyone and everything in the universe. They know it is their job to help each of us fulfill our destiny.

Anthony, too, hadn't intended to go to that club; he didn't consciously plan to meet his future wife at that noisy, dark nightclub. But his spirit guides and his soul knew what was about to go down.

Anthony and I just celebrated our 31st wedding anniversary. Every day I'm with my husband, I thank God that our souls and the spirit guides knew what our conscious minds did not.

Like you, I can't remember making the plans for my life before I was born as Kim. However, during a meditation, I once had a vision that will remain etched in my mind for years to come. In this vision, I saw myself standing in a big white conference room. In this conference room was an enormous white oval table with white chairs. Seated in the chairs were spiritual counselors—both men and women—and some elderly men. Although they were human in form, they each had a glowing light that spilled out from the perimeters of their bodies. Everyone wore stark white garments. I wore a stark white, silky robe that was cinched at my waist with a woven, gold braid. The conference room appeared to have no walls. From where I stood, there was no beginning or end to the room.

While I was in the room, I witnessed a discussion about me. I couldn't hear what was being said, but I knew they were talking about me in depth. It seemed like they were talking among themselves as if they didn't want anyone else to hear, but it was clear that they were discussing making some sort of decision about me and my progress on Earth. I don't know how I knew the gist of their conversation—I just did. They were trying to decide whether or not to promote me to a higher level, like a graduation from one level of education to another. An elderly man with a white beard was writing something on the top page of a stack of papers. He was using an inkwell and a dipping pen. I felt like I was a contestant on *American Idol* and he was the judge. Of course, I was hoping that he would give me a high score!

I believe what really happened in this meditation was that I had risen up into a spiritual dimension where I could witness what was going on around me. I still don't know the exact plan, or what score I received from those judges. Only time will tell!

Unfortunately, no one in the three-dimensional world can really tell you what is your soul purpose. I mean, some people can gently guide you to try to find it, but even then, the answers they may give you are their opinion about what path they think you should choose, not yours. And let's face it, you can't find it by asking Google or Siri. But when your consciousness begins to align with the decisions and goals made prebirth—when it aligns with the wisdom contained in your soul—you can clearly see that there is a real purpose and plan for your existence.

Many souls, perhaps some of you reading this book, are going through what is called the *awakening process* or *ascension*. To read more about ascension, please refer to the last chapter in this book. Here is the short version: During ascension, the human heart and spirit begin to wake up through the activation of the light body, also known as a higher level of consciousness. If you are confused, try picturing a beautiful light filtering in from the cosmos, touching each person's heart, rousing them from their spiritual slumber. Once the light touches us, higher frequencies rush in, raising our level of consciousness from the dense three-dimensional world of separation to a higher frequency or vibration of love, light, and oneness. This is where the term *enlightenment* comes from.

In addition to ascension, The Universe sends you to Earth with many cosmic collaborators who help you evolve. These include God Himself, who reaches through the universe, through time and space, and shows Himself to us. I'm now going to show you only a few of the infinite ways in which God sends you messages and reveals Himself. His messages illuminate the perfect connection between you, me, Himself, and The Universe.

Feel free to mark up this chapter with a highlighter pen or underline the things you wish to do further research on. Although I do not claim to be an expert in these modalities, I certainly use them to seek out information about my own soul and I suggest that you do the same.

The first thing you need to know is that we are one and the same, part of a single system created by God through what is called Sacred Geometry.

Sacred Geometry is the perfectly balanced patterns in The Universe. It reveals the harmony and oneness of The Universe, and it shows us God's hand everywhere.

Sacred Geometry has its own overseer, Archangel Metatron, who governs the magical flow of energy in geometrical patterns. Metatron is also known as the Angel of Life. In art, Metatron is usually depicted guarding the tree of life. According to a myth, his vast wisdom and power put him right after God in the spiritual hierarchy. Metatron was commissioned by God to assist humanity in evolving. He keeps the records of souls in the Book of Life (also known as the Akashic Records). He cares about you and quietly stands in the background cheering you on. One of his missions is to help you rise above the lower vibrations, which keep you stuck in a spiritual prison. This means Metatron has the giant task of helping people rise above the dark forces, so they can ascend into the heart, where the flow of the highest frequency of light and love is continuous.

Some believe that Metatron is one of the few angels who lived his life in human form. He is reputed to have been the prophet Enoch in biblical days. Because Metatron was human, he understands human challenges in a way that other angels can't. He tirelessly works with us to help us heal ourselves, both mentally and physically. My guess is that Metatron was around way before the birth of Enoch; I think he was Enoch's spirit guide, helping him throughout his life.

My gut tells me that Metatron was around when the universe was made by Infinite Intelligence, which created a map of everything that spanned in all directions of space and time. This map is known as Metatron's cube. This cube consists of 13 equal spheres with lines radiating out from the center of each, extending all the way to the centers of each of the other 12 circles. These spheres can be found in all

METATRON'S CUBE

levels of creation from the dense low physical plane all the way up to the highest vibrational frequency, or unconditional love. Each of us has the potential to connect with the 13 energy centers of Metatron's cube. Doing so helps us realize and embrace our full soul potential. Of course, Metatron is always standing nearby, willing to help light the way for your soul. He continually reminds you, in subtle ways, to ask for his help while you are trying to find your soul purpose.

Since Metatron's cube and all its geometrical shapes are the guiding force of all creation, the next time you want to witness God in motion, cut a head of celery (an entire stalk) at its base. What do you see? There's a flower! When you slice an apple horizontally—voilà, another flower! What about the perfectly sound and useful structure of a honeycomb? It's made by bees—yes, tiny buzzing things without the power of language create an incredible, complex storage unit for honey. Who showed them how to do that? God, of course! Once I've pointed out to you the patterns and shapes of Sacred Geometry, you will see the perfect structure of The Divine wherever you turn.

Sacred Geometry is intrinsically linked to our souls. It helps open our heart center, allowing love to flow through. It heals past traumas and illnesses by activating dormant DNA strands that lie in each of us, to help us achieve spiritual ascension (see chapter 11). When you are in the presence of high-frequency light patterns, your entire being shifts into a place of joy and gratitude. It is a profound experience—one you will never forget.

Most spiritual acts, meditation for example, occur on the right side of our brain. This is the creative, more flowing and open side of the brain. When we engage in a spiritual activity, the right side of our brain lights up. Have you ever left a yoga class feeling all zen? Then you hopped in your car, only to enter a heavy flow of traffic—then started screaming, maybe even cursing at the car in front of you, and immediately felt as though you had lost the peace you had created only moments ago? That's because once you left that spiritual place, you allowed your left brain—the logical, analytical, more businesslike side—to take over.

Your brain often functions like two political parties that find it difficult to work together. They can find a way to get along, but usually one likes to dominate the other. Fortunately, God found a way for our brains to "reach across the aisle": through Sacred Geometry. Geometry, like all disciplines in mathematics, is understood and processed by your left brain. Although I didn't do too well in math classes, and I probably forgot how to do a geometry equation, I do feel very connected to the sacredness of geometry. This form of geometry is related to spirituality and creation, and is understood and processed by the right brain. As a psychic medium, my right brain is well developed, as is anyone who works with the higher realms such as musicians, artists, writers, and inventors; the list is endless. When you experience Sacred Geometry, both parts of your brain are engaged together in a beautiful unity.

THE FLOWER OF LIFE

The Flower of Life is a modern name given to a symbol that appeared in permanent form—engraved and etched into marble—more than 6,000 years ago. It is a derivative of Metatron's cube: One can change into the other. (When you connect the several intersections of the Flower of Life, it turns into Metatron's cube.) The Flower of Life is also a blueprint of the universe.

The Flower of Life is a hexagonal energy grid made up of patterns of multiple overlapping circles of the same diameter. The center of each circle is on the circumference of numerous surrounding circles, and all the circles are enclosed together within a single circle. Examples of this design have been found in the Temple of Osiris at Abydos in Egypt. Leonardo da Vinci used the Flower of Life in drawings and designs. The Flower of Life means many different things to different cultures around the world. What's important is that so many diverse cultures adopted this symbol into their religion. The harmony and balance in the Flower of Life has spiritual potency: It is magical because The Universe in all its divine wisdom is magical. In the kabbalah, a system of Jewish mysticism that dates back to the beginning of Judaism, each circle in the Flower of Life represents a chakra, called *sefirot* in Hebrew (see page 132 for an image of the Tree of Life).

The Flower of Life conveys different spiritual messages to different people. Information about all matters ranging from the human body to how to build a skyscraper is hidden within the perfect pattern of the Flower of Life. No matter who you are and what culture your community is, you will be drawn to the Flower of Life. It has a balance and beauty that we naturally find appealing. Our connection to it is spiritual: It is one way of connecting to The Higher Power.

Let's look at the circles in the Flower of Life. Think about what a circle represents—it symbolizes wholeness, infinity, unity, and completion. The expression "to come full circle" means to complete the cycle of some action. When we work in a circular fashion we begin at one point on a circle and end up there too. This is like our relationship to God: We begin with Him, we go through our lives with Him, and in the end we're with Him again. But wait—there is no end, we will be with Him for eternity. The circle is a universal symbol of The God Force in many cultures and religions. Think of the halo seen in art since the beginning of modern man. What is a halo if not a circle hovering over one's head? Often halos are shown with rays of light beaming up out of them, pointing up to the heavens where we find our connection to God.

Remember when you sat at your desk in school and doodled as you listened to your teacher speak? Think about what you liked to draw. Circles? Or flowers made out of circles? I remember doodling circles upon circles upon circles. I didn't consciously realize I was drawing some form of Sacred Geometry, but I was. It relaxed me—perhaps it helped me focus. And I wasn't the only one! Many of the kids around me were doing the same thing. You might have been a doodler too, or maybe you still are. For doodlers and non-doodlers alike, I highly recommend that you draw, or trace, or color in images of Sacred Geometry.

In doing this, you create neural pathways that connect the right and left sides of your brain. When you use neural pathways over and over again, they grow deeper, so thoughts and ideas flow in the same manner as water that flows over the same curves and dips in a riverbed. When you do something often enough, your brain will automatically fall into those pathways. This is true for both good uses of our brain and bad uses. And it's one reason to break bad habits, to break up negative thinking patterns. You want to avoid negative neural pathways, while reinforcing positive neural pathways. This is what happens when you celebrate the Sacred Geometry around you.

When you bring images of Sacred Geometry into your life, you bring a better flow of energy into your life. For maximum left-and-right-brain cooperation, try copying the Flower of Life by coloring it, or drawing it. Color in different circles or arcs and find new designs, patterns, and shapes. In doing this, you will connect to this ancient and powerful symbol beyond simple visualization. You will also engage your right and left brain simultaneously, which will bring you to a higher spiritual realm and connect you in a more profound way to The God Force.

On page 130, the Flower of Life. Below, the Flower of Life rearranged as the Tree of Life.

THE TREE OF LIFE

FENG SHUI

Feng shui began more than 5,000 years ago in China. It was created in recognition of the power of Sacred Geometry. For years it was believed to be so powerful that only royal families and emperors were allowed to use it. In China, temples and palaces were built according to the Sacred Geometry of feng shui.

Prior to modern times, people instinctively knew where, and toward which cardinal point of the Earth, to set up shop and settle down. The five elements that are part of feng shui—wood, earth, water, metal, and fire—were naturally a part of their lives. There was wood in the trees, earth below their feet, water flowing nearby, metal in the rocks and caves, and fire around which they gathered each night. We were more like bees then, who know where to find the honey and where to set up the hive. But with the chaos and noise of modern life, this intuitive knowledge, given to us by God, is drowned out. When you go back to your intuitive knowledge, you go back to your soul.

The two guiding principles in feng shui are the Fibonacci sequence and the golden ratio.

The Fibonacci sequence is a series of numbers, starting with zero, that is created when you add the first two numbers to create the sum, which is the third number in the series. The sum of any two adjacent numbers is the next number. Here's the beginning of the Fibonacci sequence: 0, 1, 1, 2, 3, 5, 8, 13, 21, 34 . . . all the way to infinity. Four is not a Fibonacci number. There are patterns throughout nature that replicate the Fibonacci sequence. The way seashells spiral outward, if graphed, replicates the Fibonacci sequence. And the petals of many flowers can be numbered through the Fibonacci sequence. Flowers with four petals do exist, but they are rare—for example, finding a four-leaf clover is considered to be good luck because it is very rare and hard to come by. Whether or not you are good at math doesn't really matter. All you need to know is that the spiral designs made by this series of mathematical equations can be found in all living things.

In feng shui, each number in the Fibonacci sequence holds great power. The number one is the center. It is God—it is you and me. The number two is two parts coming together with opposite energies: yin, which is female, and yang, which is male. The number three represents the Chinese cosmic trinity of Heaven, Earth, and human Qi (pronounced *chi,* which is the life-force in each of us). For Christians, the Holy Trinity is the father (God), the son (Jesus), and the Holy Spirit (the spirit of God and Jesus as one).

The golden ratio is represented numerically as 1.618 and the Greek letter Phi. Two numbers are in the golden ratio if their ratio (the larger number divided by the smaller) is the same as the ratio of the two added together to the larger of the two. The golden ratio is related to the Fibonacci sequence in that if you take any two successive numbers in the Fibonacci sequence, their ratio is very close to the golden ratio. For example, the ratio of 13 to 21 (21 divided by 13) is 1.615. The Great Pyramids and the Parthenon have proportions of the golden ratio. The proportions of humans and other mammals also follow the golden ratio: If you measure from your navel to the floor, and from the top of your head to your navel, the ratio of those numbers usually comes out to something close to the golden ratio. Ants and honeybees also have golden-ratio proportions.

Back to feng shui! The placement of objects in a home or building is determined by the golden ratio. That is, feng shui is the practice of using Sacred Geometry to create harmony in your environment that mimics the harmony God created in the universe. The five elements named above are also worked into the home or building to create energy flow within the space and within the persons occupying the space. In fact, the very words *feng shui* mean "wind and water," a reference to the two forces continuously in motion in our lives, the two things that sustain us: wind, which is equal to air and breathing, and water, which is essential to all life-forms.

Everything in nature was designed by God and flows harmoniously in a way that can be graphed through numerical sequences. The flow created by feng shui is carried in meridians, or channels. If there is too much clutter around us, our channels become blocked. Think of a garden hose that has a kink in it—water barely drips out. The only way to release that powerful flow of water is to unlock the kink—open the hose into a loose, free-flowing structure.

Another part of this ancient practice is the use of a special kind of floor plan, also known as an energy map or *bagua.* Translated from the

Chinese language, this word means eight areas or sections. Visually, bagua areas are laid out in the shape of an octagon and not only are arranged to correspond to different areas in a person's life, but are also carefully mapped out to allow energy to flow in and out of their space (office or home) effortlessly. Note that the bagua map is not a literal floor plan; it's only a mental construct and should be used as a guideline to use your physical space as an anchor to help you focus on and manifest the energy you want to attract into your life. There are two basic bagua maps: 1) the traditional or classic compass bagua and 2) the three-door gate of chi bagua. You can learn more about these two methods of placement in your spare time, but for the purpose of this chapter, I am using the three-door gate of chi bagua. First you must find the front of your house before you can determine which areas of the chart should go where. For example: The wealth area of your home or workplace should be the furthest area on the left from the door. If you would like to make a bagua map and place it over the floor plans of your home or office, get a plain piece of paper and fold it in thirds and then in thirds the other direction; you come up with nine square boxes. Copy the chart on the following page when determining areas and placement. As already mentioned, each of the eight areas of the bagua map contain one of the five elements of the cycle of life: wood, earth, water, metal, and fire, and each has a corresponding topic and color. The most important area is the center of the bagua, and it represents balance, health, and the self. Earth tones such as yellows and browns are usually used in this center space to bring stability and grounding into your life. See the chart on the following page for further information on other area placements, as well as their corresponding element and color.

Yes, it's true: Our surroundings have a part in what we attract into our lives. In trying to find your soul purpose, it's important that you don't block out any universal goodness or blessings that are trying to make their way to you.

The way we tend to the spaces around us can represent how we feel in our bodies and souls. And the arrangement of the spaces around us can affect how we feel. Our bodies and mind respond to our environment. And the flow of energy within us (the meridians) responds to what's around us.

THREE-DOOR GATE OF CHI BAGUA

SE   SW

NE   NW

Purple
Wealth
Abundance
Wood

Red
Fame
Fire

Pink
Relationships
Marriage
Earth

Green
Family
Past
Wood

Yellow

Earth   Self

Center

White
Children
Creativity
Metal

Blue/Green
Knowledge
Spirituality
Water

Black
Career
Water

Gray
Helpful People
Travel
Metal

Door   Door   Door

Entrance   Entrance   Entrance

SOUL KIT

Making Room for New Energy

The art of feng shui encourages a harmonious flow of energy (chi) moving through all objects in your environment. As humans, we tend to get attached to items we've acquired, and very rarely do we part with our favorite collections. Whether or not you realize it, we do the same with unfavorable emotions that we carry around inside us, holding us hostage on a subconscious level. We carry these emotions around like an old, worn-out suitcase that we forgot to unpack. It has been said that your outer world is like a mirror that reflects your inner world. By following these three easy steps, you will open up blockages and declutter your environment, creating sacred space on the outside as well as on the inside.

1. Start by cleaning out one room in your home that you spend the most time in, such as your bedroom. Begin by cleaning out small drawers. Make three piles: One pile should consist of items that you haven't used in six months—label this pile *DONATIONS*. Try to keep in mind that your trash may become someone else's treasures. Once you realize that these items will make someone else happy, it won't be too difficult to let go of them. The second pile should consist of any items that are no longer useful to anyone—label this pile *TRASH*. Try to remember a time in your life when these items were useful to you and brought you joy. Honor the memories and release them to make room for new items that will bring you more joy. The third pile should consist of items that you do use and plan to keep—label this pile *KEEP*.

2. Once you are done sorting through the piles, make sure you organize the items labeled *KEEP* and neatly place them back in their respective drawers. Quickly pack up the items from the other two piles and make arrangements to dispose of them as soon as possible. You will feel lighter in no time. You will quickly feel motivated to tackle cleaning out the rest of your room, and finally the rest of your home. In doing so, make

the same three piles and follow through accordingly. Ahhh—doesn't that feel good?

3. Take a look around your bedroom. Make sure there is nothing blocking the door into your room. If you have big, bulky pieces of furniture that are too big for the space, try to find another home for them. Remember, less is more. Place your bed against the wall that is diagonal from your bedroom door. If this is not possible, pick a wall that will accommodate a good solid headboard (for grounding) and a nightstand placed on each side of the bed to balance the energy. Try not to store items under your bed, since it blocks energy flow. Add a pretty, colored rug under or around your bed for further grounding.

4. Feng shui works hand in hand with the **Law of Attraction.** Create a vision board and fill it with pictures of what you intend to attract into your life. For example: If you would like to attract a partner to spend your life with, look for a picture in a magazine of a happy couple who are kissing in front of the Eiffel Tower. (You get the idea.) Place the picture on your vision board and hang it where you can see it frequently.

5. Also hang pictures of items that make you happy and that are pleasing to the eye—preferably items that connect to the elements of the Earth that can energize you. Also, you may want to add plants, rocks, crystals, or candles. Bring in the element of water with a fountain, one that circulates water with a small pump. The sound of the water can help you relax as your drift off to sleep.

You know from chapter 4 that in order to open your heart chakra and the chakras above the heart, you need to clear away the clutter so that the light can penetrate. In feng shui, the chakras are the Qi, the life-force that needs to be clean and balanced for the energy to flow through you and out of you. But feng shui goes beyond the body and says that it's just as important that we open and declutter our homes and work areas for the energy to flow through.

Using all the elements of feng shui—the golden triangle, the five elements, and the referenced chart—you can open the flow of Qi in your life, open your chakras, and bring forth all the great and beautiful abundance of The Universe. In opening yourself up and bringing forth all these gifts, your soul purpose will shine out of you like a beautiful spotlight.

Your bedroom is only one expression of the love you give to yourself. Increase the love you have for yourself and others by letting go of negative thought patterns and emotions that you have been storing inside you like old, clunky golf clubs that fall out of the closet every time you open the door. Practice the *Light Meditation* technique, found on pages 25–26. This meditation will serve as feng shui for your soul. Relax and enjoy it.

Now that you have created a clean and tranquil environment on the outside, as well as on the inside, energy around you can now flow more easily. Sit back and watch it flow its way directly to you, bringing forth all of your dreams and aspirations.

9

It's a Numbers Game: Understanding the Universal Language of Numbers and Why They Hold the Power to Positively Influence Your Life

> *"Numbers are the highest degree of knowledge—*
> *it is knowledge itself."*
> —PLATO

NUMEROLOGY IS a term that you may have heard about, but up until this point, may not have had the chance to learn much about. Simply put, numerology is the study of numbers in and around a person's life, and since each number holds a certain vibration, a person's personal numbers can reveal a great deal about their personality and general characteristics. Numbers create harmony, balance, and pattern. They are used for everything from building cities to curing cancer. Numbers exist outside of us. That is, even if we weren't here to count and use numbers, they would still be part of God's blueprint for the universe. Used correctly, numerology can change your life.

When you choose to understand number patterns, and the meaning behind them, you are also choosing to push yourself closer to understanding your soul purpose. In this chapter, you will learn the meaning of important numbers as they apply to your life, as well as the basic principles surrounding numerology. Since numerology is based on mathematical calculations, you will learn an easy way to determine important numbers, such as your Life Path Number and your Soul Urge Number. You will learn how to recognize Master Numbers and number sequences when they show up in your life as spiritual messages designed to help guide you to follow the map of your soul to greater self-awareness and discovery. Don't worry, you don't need to be a math wizard to follow along.

Have you ever noticed that certain numbers show up repeatedly? Maybe even daily! You may see a certain pattern of numbers over and over again on a digital clock, license plates, or grocery store receipts. When someone is trying to convey a message to us from the great beyond, they can be very clever in the ways in which they do so. I receive the number 444 daily in one form or another. On my way home from being out of town, I stopped to get gas, and guess how much a pack of cigarettes at the gas station cost? That's right: $4.44. Although I do not smoke and never have, I couldn't help but notice the life-size banner advertising a sale with my favorite numbers.

At one point, during a very difficult time in my life, the number 444 was showing up for me so often that I knew I was being directed to research this phenomenon. When I learned of its meaning, I cried tears of joy. It turns out that when three or more 4s appear, this is God's way of letting you know He has sent His angels to watch over you, expressing their love through their presence. They are telling you that you are resonating with The Universe in perfect synchronicity. When you pray, do you ever wonder if you're being heard? If you find a pattern of 4s, you can know for certain that your prayers are being heard and angels are helping you realize your goals. You are not alone; you are being divinely guided. Now, how cool is that? I promise, the spirits will bring your attention to the 4s when you most need it. They're hearing you now, but they might not let you know until your darkest moments. When you see the same patterns in numbers over and over again, you are receiving messages from The Universe. So when I saw the price of cigarettes the other day, I knew I'd have a safe journey home.

Some numbers were chosen by and for you when you were figuring out your name and birthdate before you were born. Believe it or not, each letter of your name carries a specific vibration, and so does each number of your birth month, date, and year. When calculations are done based on your personal numbers, you can learn about certain habits, patterns, and behaviors by understanding the meaning of these numbers. It is important to note that numerology does not necessarily predict a person's future. However, through the powerful vibrations of numbers, people can fine-tune negative aspects of their personality, rise above challenges, and unlock secret codes to reach their highest potential. By letting the numbers increase your level of awareness and consciousness, you can then develop a better plan for your life by making the necessary changes or adjustments.

In numerology, your Life Path Number is typically reflective of who you are and describes your traits and personality—it is akin to your sun sign in astrology. Many believe that your Life Path Number is the most important one, since it reveals certain gifts and talents you were born with, as well as illuminates any challenges you were born to face—along with the soul lessons you are meant to follow.

It is very easy to calculate your Life Path Number: All you need is your full birthday (month, day, and year). I will calculate my Life Path Number for you here so you can see how it's done. My birthday is June 2, 1964. First, you must reduce each number to a single digit. June is the sixth month, so we will start with the number **6**. The second digit is the day of the month when you were born. I was born on the 2nd, so we must add the number **2**. So far, we have 8. Now I must add up the numbers of the year to create a single number. $1 + 9 + 6 + 4 = 20$, and then 20 is reduced to $2 + 0 = 2$. Now we add them all up: 6 (month) + 2 (day) + 2 (reduced year) = 10. When I reduce the number 10 to a single digit, I get my Life Path Number: **1**.

Master Numbers: There are three magical numbers in numerology: 11, 22, and 33. These three numbers do not get reduced to a single digit. They carry the highest vibration of all the numbers and are often referred to as the *Triangle of Enlightenment*. When these numbers appear as your core number, or anywhere else in your life, such as your house number, it must be understood that your soul has come here to master many spiritual truths. Unfortunately, as good as this sounds, it can be both a blessing and a curse. It can be difficult to have a Master Number because where there are more opportunities to become your own guru, more challenges often follow. It requires great time and effort to understand how to incorporate the power of a Master Number into one's life and personality. But it is definitely worth the effort!

There are various types of core numbers used in numerology. Besides your Life Path Number, the Soul Urge Number (also called the Heart's Desire Number) is one you came up with before you entered this life. This number represents your heart's desire and reflects your inner life. Now, you may be thinking, *Who doesn't know their own heart's desire?* The answer to that is *Many people!* When we listen to our egos, and the egos of others, in our day-to-day lives, we block our chakras and shut out the light radiating from our souls. When we block our heart chakra long enough, we lose touch with our soul and forget what our heart's desire is. Focusing on your Soul Urge Number is one way to understand yourself better. This number will show you your true feelings and the intentions behind your actions. It will help you be true to yourself. Below I will give you the formula to help you find your Soul Urge Number so that you may get started on changing your life and living your soul purpose.

To begin, look at the chart below: It gives a numerical value for each letter in the alphabet. Take your first, middle, and last name (given to you at birth), and add up the numeric values of the vowels in each. *Do this for each name separately, reducing them to a single digit.* When you are finished gathering the numeric value of each name, add them all together. Once you have the sum of each name, reduce the number to a single digit. *That*, my friends, is your Heart's Desire Number. It was with you at birth and it will be with you to the end. Look closely and see how and when that number appears to you; how and when it leads you to your heart's desire and your soul purpose.

1	2	3	4	5	6	7	8	9
A	B	C	D	E	F	G	H	I
J	K	L	M	N	O	P	Q	R
S	T	U	V	W	X	Y	Z	

As previously mentioned, vibration is a universal language, expressed by numbers in geometric ratios and patterns that define color (spectrums of light), sound, and form. Although the number zero is hardly used in a numerology calculation, make no mistake about it: This number is of great significance and holds tremendous power in the universe. When zero is added to any number, it gives it greater value. In our monetary system, the more zeros we have after any number, the better—right? Vibrationally, the number zero, shaped as a circle, has no beginning and no end and represents both the male and the female form of all that lives. With zero we are back to Sacred Geometry, Metatron's cube, and the Flower of Life. As I've said before, the circle—also zero—represents eternity and The God Force, or The Source of All Creation.

Even as the zero stands on its own in our number system, the single digits 1 through 9 are the foundation used by most numerologists today. Each of these numbers holds a unique vibration and has a different power and meaning. The meanings behind these numbers vary slightly but are fairly universal in different cultures and religions. When you read the meaning behind these numbers given below, keep in mind that the meaning can be applied not only to your life path, but to the life cycle you are currently in. (As the number of the year changes each year, so, too, will your life cycle number change.) If you see any sequence of numbers reappearing in your life, check and see what message the numbers are trying to offer you. Numbers are similar to people in that each has a personality all its own. In what follows, I will describe each number as if it were a person.

Number 1: To be number one is to be a leader, an innovator, an achiever, and a trailblazer. One is singular and represents independence. Even the symbol of 1 has a regal stance (or maybe it's more like a disciplined soldier standing at attention, ready to take action). Although Ones stand out, they also stand alone and need to figure things out on their own. Ones are self-assured and energetic—they often lead us and teach us. Because the number one is the first upright number (following zero) in sequence, it represents starts, or new beginnings. If you see the number one popping up repeatedly in your life, your angels and guides are telling you to leave the past behind and make a fresh start. These angels will guide your path with purity and love.

Number 2: The number two means unity. You know the expressions *Two heads are better than one* and *Two peas in a pod.* The number two forces us to have our own identity while joining with a partner to combine our gifts and talents for the betterment of mankind. The number two promotes communication and harmony and helps us learn more about ourselves, especially how to create more balance through duality. We would never know any other opinions but our own if we didn't interact with other people. Twos are humble and of service to others. Even the shape of the 2 resembles a person on bended knees with his head bowed. If you see patterns with the number two, your angels are sending you a message to have faith and courage. They want you to know your prayers have been heard and that, though things may not look too promising at the current time, your angels are helping you behind the scenes to manifest your deepest desires. You are not alone when Two is by your side.

Number 3: The number three represents this very dimension in which we live (the third dimension). Nature appears to us in threes: the sun, moon, and stars; gas, liquid, and solid; height, width, and depth. Customarily, we do things in threes in order to manifest our desires and bring them into our physical reality. The number three is recurrent in folktales and myth: three wishes to be made to the genie, three little pigs, three bears, three strikes and you're out in baseball. It is one of the strongest numbers; people influenced by the number three resonate with joy and optimism. Threes are movers and shakers; they're also great storytellers. Because of their impeccable communication skills, Threes make great teachers or lecturers. They are creative and intuitive and exude positive energy. Although they have a very happy demeanor, a Three who is still working on ascending to the highest expression of their vibration can be insecure and overly emotional, and lack focus.

If you consistently notice the number three around you, it is a call from the heavens, reminding you to reconnect by plugging back into Source energy. Seeing threes can indicate that highly evolved masters are working on your behalf and are teaching you how to become more spiritually attuned to their world. If you're seeing threes in your life, rest assured the ascended masters are dropping into your dream state too, giving you lesson plans for life. Lucky you!

Number 4: The shape of the number 4 says it all. With its harsh, linear edges, all wrapped up in itself, the shape of a four can leave little room for energy to flow—little room for change or compromise. However, people who are influenced by the number four are goal-oriented and driven by their passion. They don't take the easy route; they live in their minds and allow logic to motivate them. Since logic is derived from the left side of the brain, Fours seldom explore the right side of their brains, where creativity and inspiration dwell. They are hard on themselves and are perfectionists. Practicality is a Four's middle name. With unwavering Fours, what you see is what you get.

I would say that Fours are very similar to Virgos—driving ahead with a goal in mind but still grounded, reliable, and trustworthy. I've already described the power of consecutive fours, like the ones that appear to me daily. I hope they appear to you too, showing you that angels are always with you and standing by, ready to help you achieve your goals. Follow the sign when you see it. After all, who doesn't want a little help from angels—what have you got to lose by following their lead?

Number 5: Five is the number of risk, change, and growth. People who are influenced by the number five are good at so many things that they often have a hard time deciding which path they wish to take. Fives need to be careful not to be the jack-of-all-trades, but master of none. They struggle between their heads and their hearts. They love their freedom and seldom like to commit if it will keep them from experiencing the many pleasures they seek. Fives are smart, they have great ideas, and they can be a positive influence on others. On the flip side, they are often restless and rarely sit still long enough to find their core and focus. Fives must focus on balance and discipline in order to succeed. When the number five consistently appears in your life, the angels are trying to ease you into embracing positive changes. They want to remind you to keep your eye on the prize, and with their help, along with hard work, dedication, and faith, you are well on your way to finding true happiness.

Number 6: The number six is the number of creation and stability. It is also about finding balance and responsibility and being of service to others. Sixes are very nurturing and can be more concerned for the welfare of others over themselves. Because Sixes feel the need to fix everything, they must also be careful not to enable the people they love by robbing them of their life lessons. They are over-givers and want to give love as much as they want to receive it. The symbol of the number 6 has been said to look like a mother's womb (filled with love, and creating through love). Sixes came here to learn how to find their gifts through creation and to share their gifts through service to others. They make great mothers, life coaches, therapists, and nurses.

Sixes must always strive to remain grounded in order to maintain stability. If they don't find balance, they can get so caught up in helping others, that their lives can begin to unravel. Don't worry if you see more than one six in your travels. Sixes appear when things seem to be out of control in your life and your angels want to help you to rearrange your priorities. Usually, when you see sixes, your angels want you to slow down to see all the blessings around you. They also want you to pay more attention in your home, to nurture yourself and your family more. If you remain in gratitude, with an open heart, the number six can be one of your best friends.

Number 7: The shape of the number 7 cuts on every angle. This is the favorite number of most people, since it is considered lucky. It's a number that can teach us many spiritual lessons. Sevens were born in search of faith in themselves and others. They have psychic abilities and a direct connection to the higher realms. People who are influenced by the number seven must find the balance between the material and spiritual worlds. They march to the beat of their own drum, and they create their own perceptions of reality. They often live inside their minds, so they can convince themselves that that is the safest place to be, when in fact it only isolates them from the outside world. Sevens make great researchers, philosophers, and mystics, since they are always seeking truth and knowledge. Because seven is such a spiritual number, it imparts messages and paths to The Divine. Your angels will allow the number seven to appear frequently in your space to let you know they are helping you move closer to your divine nature and the mission of your soul.

Number 8: The shape of the number 8 is two circles in motion, one spilling into the other. On its side, the number eight represents infinity. Eight has infinite power and strength when it rises into higher consciousness. On Earth, in the three-dimensional reality, Eights have a balancing act to perform as they try to use their power in the lower levels. The phrase *slow and steady* comes to mind in describing the vibration of the number eight. Eights are always on the move, trying to strive for more. They want to learn more, see more, do more, and have more, since they are never satisfied with what they already have. Their lesson is to slow down and appreciate what they have in the moment, and to pull their power from the spiritual realm, where it resides, and not from their ego.

Eights have superior managerial abilities and are fearless when it comes to taking on big projects or titles. You'll find Eights overseeing the construction of skyscrapers or running high-tech companies in Silicon Valley. The confidence and know-it-allness of an Eight makes them blunt and sometimes tactless. There is a lot of karmic energy attached to eights. If you see more than one eight around you, angels are signaling you that prosperity is yours to take, but first you must seek balance. Like the symbol of infinity, flowing with no beginning and no end, there is no limit to the blessings you can receive through the number eight.

Number 9: The number nine has the qualities of all the numbers, one through eight. If you add all these numbers, you get 36, which is reduced to 9 (3 + 6 = 9). People who are influenced by the number nine are seeking Heaven on Earth. They are the humanitarians of the world, seeking spiritual truths. Nines want to spread the light to others and expect nothing in return. They are the Mother Teresas of the world. Emotionally, things are often hard for Nines, since they find it difficult to live in the harsh, three-dimensional world. Nines are smart and can make money easily, but they aren't motivated by money except to give it to charity. Angels send you the number nine to remind you that they are always ready to assist you in letting go of negativity, so that you may ascend to the highest vibration of love with your compassionate heart.

Zero through nine are not the only powerful numbers in the universe. There are many others, though some stand out: 12, for example, is a number worth talking about. There are 187 mentions of the number 12 in the Bible. In all examples of 12 there is completeness and purpose. The number can be seen as representing a whole. There are 12 months in the year, 12 signs in the Zodiac, 12 eggs in a dozen, 12 hours in a day, 12 hours in a night, 12 steps in recovery programs, 12 grades in school, 12 inches in a foot, 12 apostles. If you add the numbers 1 and 2 together, you get the number 3 (the trinity). Since God has deemed 12 special, so should you.

The number 40 is also powerful and appears in the Bible 146 times. Even if you've never read the Bible, 40 is a number you'll find to have significance.

In noticing these numbers, seeing the power they hold in their completeness, you are connecting to the infinite wisdom of The Divine and moving closer to your soul purpose.

SOUL KIT

Keeping Track of Numbers

Carry a journal with you for seven days. Whenever you get a free moment, write down the numbers that have appeared to you, in any form, throughout the day. When you are stopped at a traffic light in your car you may notice the license plate in front of you has numbers that match your birthday. Or perhaps you are waking up at the same time every night and realize that the time on the clock matches the time your loving grandmother departed from this world. Yes, this is indeed a message from your grandma. Keep looking around for numbers that pop out and grab your attention, and at the end of the week, look for patterns and repetitions. What are the numbers that most often appeared over the week?

If you worked out the formulas for your Life Path Number and your Soul Urge Number, see how many times these numbers appeared in your space over the course of the week. If you keep seeing the same numbers in different places, especially in your dream state, perhaps you may want to try your luck and buy a Lotto ticket and pick these numbers to win. The Universe is on your side and is abundant enough to reward you. Different numbers will come to you at different times in your life. Using the information in this chapter, try to decipher what messages these numbers are holding for you.

10

The Sky Is Not the Limit!
Reaching for the Stars Through the Art
of Astrology and Learning to Shine
as Bright as Your Sun Sign

> *"I will love the light for it shows me the way, yet I*
> *will endure the darkness for it shows me the stars."*
> —OG MANDINO

ASTROLOGY HAS been around for more than 2,000 years. In the beginning, it was the same as astronomy—a complete study of the cycles of planets and cosmic events in the sky. Whether you follow it or not, it has been a part of your life in ways you don't realize. The Farmers' Almanac has always used it to determine the growing and harvest cycles for plants. Everything in nature uses astrology, in fact, to determine when to drop leaves, when to sprout flowers, to spawn, to swim upstream, to lay eggs, to fly south, to build a nest, to hibernate. All that information is conveyed according to where the planets are in the sky, how close we are to the sun, and how long the days are.

True astrology uses mathematics and astronomy to make predictions and better understand the ways of people born at particular times. It is part of Sacred Geometry. For each birth, the gravitational force of the moon is stronger or weaker, the number of hours of sunshine are more or fewer, and the diet your mother ate while you were in the womb was dictated by the foods that were in season at the time. (This is true less and less with foods being shipped around the world overnight.) That diet provided different nutrients that fed different systems in your body. The amount of sunshine and vitamin D your mother got determined her health, and yours in turn. The energy and vibrations in the world were a particular way at that time and, since we are all made up of energy, your mother—and you in the womb— responded to that energy force and those vibrations.

Your birth chart, or horoscope, is a unique map that reveals where each of the planets and other key celestial points were located at the moment of your birth. You, along with your spirit guides, strategically picked this unique combination of planetary placements before you were born. You knew the influence each planet would hold, and how these influences would assist you in rising above your Earthly challenges to help you ascend to the highest frequency.

There are many forms of astrology that can help you find purpose and meaning in your life. However, when we look to our horoscopes in newspapers or magazines, the form of astrology most commonly used today in Western culture often refers only to your sun sign: You only have to know your birthdate to find it. The sun in astrology is a mirror of the *self*. It can represent both the ego (the part of the self that is stuck in high school values) or it can represent The Higher Self (your soul purpose, or the part of the self that has graduated with a PhD!).

In reflecting you, your sun sign shows your essential life-force and vitality. It's the means by which you're meant to shine out in the world in this lifetime. A person's sun sign is what most people identify themselves with when asked, "Hey, baby, what's your sign?" (I always laugh and think of Austin Powers when I hear those words. Mike Myers nailed it—that used to be the biggest pickup line around.)

In the science of astrology, there are 12 astrological signs (there it is, that number 12 again!) in a person's chart, based on the constellations that ran along an ecliptic on the day you were born. The ecliptic is a line that marks the path of the sun during a one-year period, as seen from

Earth. What determines a person's sun sign at the time of their birth depends on which constellation the sun is passing through. Beyond one's sun sign, the ecliptic also marks the line along which the moon, planets, and asteroids travel. The constellation behind each of these at the date, time, and location of your birth determines your unique horoscope.

The 12 astrological signs are divided into four elements that represent The Universe: earth, air, fire, and water. Each element has three signs oriented to it. Look at the chart below and find your sun sign, with the corresponding symbol. Then read on in this chapter so you can learn the basic attributes of people born under each sun sign. I highly recommend you go to the library, or on the internet, and conduct more research into your sign. Anything that tells you about you, the nature of you, can guide you inwardly to self-discovery—and it can lead you to your soul purpose.

In my case, I totally understand why I decided to be born when the sun was traveling through the constellation of Gemini. The traits of a Gemini truly fit my personality. Geminis are known to be very social and communicative: two qualities I need as a teacher and speaker. But Gemini also has a twin, or opposite side, which makes them thoughtful, pensive, and inward-looking. Those are the traits I need to have as a medium who gives readings to people.

Of course, my husband, Anthony, jokes from time to time about me having two sides. He says he never knows which side of me he will come home to. He admits that it makes for an exciting life. And it also keeps him on his toes. Anthony is a Virgo. Virgos are typically very grounded and easygoing. They are also known to be reliable and calm. Anthony's Virgo qualities make for a sturdy home base to support the more airy Gemini that I am. Of course, our spirit guides knew this when they pushed Anthony and me to meet. They knew exactly when each of us had entered our bodies—they knew our sun signs (and more!) and that is why they knew that in this life we would be a perfect match.

I once received an astrological reading from a woman who told me that I am like a kite, always flying high, reaching into higher dimensions. She continued by saying that Anthony is the string, tugging on the kite when he thinks I need to come back down to Earth. She hit the nail on the head. Anthony truly is a grounding force, not only for me, but for my entire family. Gotta love those Virgos.

In determining the map of one's soul, the sun sign is only one-third of the three-part equation in reading your sign. The additional components in a birth chart are the moon sign and the rising sign. The moon sign, which changes every two and a half days, is also calculated by your birthday, but it's different for people within the same sun sign. The moon represents your inner emotional self and what you need in this lifetime to feel safe, nurtured, and balanced. It's also how you nurture others.

The rising sign, or ascendant, is calculated by the exact date, time, and location of your birth. It's not dictated by a planet but instead by an important angle on your birth chart found at the 9 o'clock position. Your rising sign represents how you come across to others when you first meet them. You may have heard the expression *You only have one chance to make a good first impression.* Well, your ascendant may be a contributing factor in how good of an impression you make, or how you portray yourself to others. The ascendant reflects everything you learned during your upbringing and how you appear outwardly, both emotionally and physically. If you were conditioned or influenced to present yourself as someone other than who you truly are, then your ascendant can function as a camouflage to your true nature. In fact, many astrologers view the ascendant as the masks we wear in public.

In having a basic understanding of our sun, moon, and rising signs, we can gain a deeper insight to our very souls. Follow along as I share with you a glimpse into my personal zodiac.

As you already know, I'm a Gemini—that's my sun sign. My moon is in Pisces and my ascendant, or rising sign, is Cancer. These three powers together create a much clearer picture of me than simply Gemini, my sun sign. The meaning of all three powers together is that I'm ruled by intuition. Boy, is that ever right! I'm also sensitive and empathetic to other people and the forces around me. Again, what is a medium if not someone with those qualities? These signs also tag me as someone who is both affectionate and critical. Affectionate, yes, and critical—well, mostly toward myself. I have to admit that *not* being critical is something I've been working on for years. It wasn't until I saw it in my astrology that I could see it in myself. And once I could see it in myself, I could work on letting go of it—opening my heart chakra and giving out love instead of criticism.

Being charitable is another trait of people with my three signs. As you know, I am a teacher; teaching is one of the most charitable professions. When I share my gifts, and teach others to find their gifts, I really am acting in full accordance with my sun sign, my moon sign, and my ascending sign.

If you choose to have an astrologer read more into your astrological chart, then be sure to find a trusted and reputable astrologer who understands the placement of the planets. Get references and interview them. Look for the real deal and avoid the phonies! Most astrologers today have advanced computer programs designed to create your personal birth chart in an instant. All you need to know is your birthday, birth time, and place of birth, and the computer does the calculations. If you don't know that information, and your birth parents can't tell you, then go in the attic and dig up your birth certificate in that dusty box that also holds your original social security card and maybe a few old report cards. Your birth certificate should have your time of birth on it. And if you can't find your birth certificate, you can find all the information in the records of the hospital where you were born. I really do recommend that you go to the trouble to find all this: The planets can help tell the story of your soul purpose.

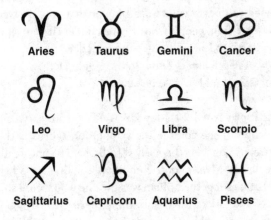

Look at the chart above and find your sun sign. On the following pages is a description of each sign. Keep in mind that each sign has a polarity of positive and negative traits. At times, we possess both the positive and negative attributes of our signs. When we're housed in a physical body, it's our goal to transcend the negative attributes and to reach our soul's goal to better reflect the positive attributes of our astrological sign. Just as the planets revolve around the sun, our soul purpose is derived from the sun in our natal charts.

Aries (born March 21–April 19): Aries is a fire sign and is depicted as a ram's curving horns. Aries is the first sign of the zodiac. People born under the sign of Aries are often considered go-getters, leaders, and pioneers. They are courageous and energetic. They are very magnetic—people are drawn to them and their great sense of adventure. If you want to get a party started, invite an Aries. If you want to start a campaign, get an Aries to lead it. Even though they can initiate any campaign, have no problem soliciting followers, and love to control every part of the campaign, Aries often don't finish what they start. So, they need the backup of someone like a Virgo to keep them to their goals.

On the negative side, Aries tend to have big egos. They're proud and they're stubborn—two traits that don't help anyone anywhere. They can be pushy and rude, especially when they have a strong opinion about something. You can count on your Aries friend to tell you that you need to update your wardrobe, or that you are wearing too much makeup. Often, people who are born under the sun sign of Aries are here on Earth to learn humility and patience.

Famous Aries include Elton John, Hugh Hefner, Leonardo da Vinci, Lady Gaga, and Maya Angelou.

Taurus (born April 20–May 20): Taurus is an earth sign and is the second sign of the zodiac. The symbol for Taurus is the head of a bull. Taureans consider themselves to be patient but, really, they're stubborn as bulls! My school friend Jillian is a Taurus. When we sold Girl Scout cookies together, Jillian was the one who would stop anyone on the street and talk to them until they'd agreed to buy a box. People born under this sign do not take no for an answer and do not like to compromise. It's their way, or the highway! Taureans are afraid of any sort of lack and can spend a lifetime accumulating wealth and material items to make themselves feel safe and worthy.

On a positive note, Taurus people are reliable, patient, stable, and practical. And, like Jillian selling Girl Scouts cookies, they are excellent at achieving their goals. It has been said that the soul lesson for a Taurus is this: Whatever they need to feel happy and content cannot be obtained by any outside source such as wealth or property. The source of great joy is inside, where all their power and strength reside. Once they figure this out, the world is truly their oyster.

Famous people born under Taurus include George Clooney, David Beckham, Adele, Queen Elizabeth II, and William Shakespeare.

Gemini (born May 21–June 20): Gemini is an air sign and is the third sign of the zodiac. The symbol for this sign is a picture of the twins. Twins can be two of the same thing or two parts of a whole, like a yin-yang symbol. Geminis are able to see both sides of any situation (the yin and the yang), and they can easily explain the broader picture to those who can't see both sides. Like other air signs, Geminis can glide like the wind. This allows them to rise above the drama and go with the flow. Gemini is my sign, as you know. Some days I float in the clouds with the spirits, and some days I'm in my kitchen obsessively looking at paint chips for the family room walls. Either way, the driving force behind Gemini is their mind—their thoughts are always spinning.

Since Gemini is ruled by the planet Mercury (the planet of communication), a Gemini can talk to you about anything and everything. As long as the conversation offers new bits of information, you will have the full attention of a Gemini. Geminis are the researchers and journalists of the zodiac, always poking and prodding for new information to add to their store. And, if curiosity didn't kill the cat, it may wind up doing some damage to a Gemini.

One of the negative traits of a Gemini is that they get bored easily and often don't stay on task. Okay, okay, guilty as charged, but I'm working on it! Geminis usually keep their pains and anguishes to themselves because they don't like to dampen the mood of those around them. However, keeping these negative emotions to themselves can often lead to anxiety and depression for the otherwise jolly Gem. If your Gemini friend who is typically bubbly demonstrates a side that you do not recognize, make sure you plan an evening of fun and laughter. You will soon see your friend return to his or her old self. No Gemini can resist a party or a social gathering (again, guilty as charged). The common soul lesson for a Gemini is to learn how to focus on one thing at a time and to live in the moment.

Famous Geminis include Sigmund Freud, Marilyn Monroe, Angelina Jolie, John F. Kennedy, and Anderson Cooper.

Cancer (born June 21–July 22): Cancer, the fourth sign of the zodiac, is a water sign. The symbol for Cancer is the crab, which is depicted by the number 69 placed sideways. The image suggests crab claws gripping onto something desirable. Cancer doesn't let go too easily! Since the moon rules the tides of the ocean, so does it rule the feelings of a Cancerian. And like the tides, the Cancer's emotions go in and out, ebbing and flowing, making them very emotional people. Sometimes the tide is high and they are happy crabs! And sometimes the tide is low and they are pessimistic or depressed. Cancers are very loving people but, boy, do they get their feelings hurt easily! Good thing those feelings change as rapidly as the tides. My friend Diane is a Cancer, and if I make her laugh just once, the whole evening becomes easy and fun.

Those born under the sign of the Crab are homebodies. Cancers like the security of being in their own comfy environment, their shell, surrounded by those they love and who love them back. They'd rather stay at home, whip up a homemade meal, and watch a classic movie with their family or friends, than go out on the town. Even if they're invited to the nicest restaurant on someone else's dime, the Cancer would rather go home and fend for him- or herself. They are the ultimate nurturers of the zodiac and can act as everyone's parent. A Cancer who loves you will love you for life. But just as you wouldn't want to defy a strict parent, you don't want to cross a Cancer! They will either retreat into their shell or lash out and sting.

The soul lesson for a Cancer is to love and nurture themselves as much as, if not more than, they nurture others. Also, Cancers need to release the negative emotions that drain them of their energy and learn how to forgive past hurts. Every Cancer needs reminding that once they embrace divinity, the love they will experience from The God Force will provide all the great strength, safety, and security they've been searching for since birth. As it is for all of us, God's love will make them whole.

Famous Cancers include Helen Keller, Nelson Mandela, Robin Williams, and Princess Diana.

Leo (born July 23–August 22): Leo is a fire sign and is the fifth sign of the zodiac. The symbol of Leo is depicted by the mane and curved spine of a lion. Since the sign of Leo is ruled by the sun, and the sun offers boundless energy and vitality, most Leos I know are always on the go, spreading positive vibes wherever they land. Leos have infectious personalities, love the limelight, and are natural entertainers. Their need to be the center of attention can sometimes swing toward narcissism and ego. They wield power in every circle, but their lion-sized egos can lead them to abuse that power. If they are a balanced Leo, they have high standards, know who they are, and are very proud of it.

A well-balanced Leo can be an inspiration to others. They are great leaders for those who lack motivation or are driven by fear. Leos know how to get the job done, they're not afraid to get their hands dirty, and they thrive on both their accomplishments and the accolade and respect of others. The soul lesson of a Leo is usually to transcend the ego, which gives them the illusion of Earthly power. A Leo who taps into their true power source—love over domination, humility over ego—can soar to the greatest heights of success. When the power of love overrides the need for power, the Leo is on the fast track to true enlightenment.

Famous Leos include Neil Armstrong, Madonna, Jennifer Lopez, President Obama, and Fidel Castro.

Virgo (born August 23–September 22): Virgo is an Earth sign and is the sixth sign of the zodiac. The constellation of Virgo in the sky is pretty easy to see on a dark night: It's a maiden carrying a shaft of wheat in one hand and fire in the other. Since Virgo is an Earth sign, Virgos are known to be very grounded. They're often described as salt of the Earth. They are easygoing and fun, but they are also committed to having a meaningful and purposeful life. An overall theme of a Virgo's soul is to be of service to others. It is no wonder the Virgo symbol offers wheat to feed and fire to keep warm. In their commitment to service, many

Virgos will put their lives on the line. My Virgo husband, Anthony, is a volunteer firefighter. This is a typical occupation of Virgos, along with other service professions like police officers, teachers, nurses, or doctors.

Two of my three sons are Virgos as well. They're in their 20s now and already live in service to others. Both of my Virgo sons have confessed that they are sounding boards for many of their coworkers and friends, who often reach out to them for solid advice. If you want the job done right, leave it to the Virgo in your life. They are the most capable of anyone in the zodiac. Virgos have high intelligence, they are organized, and they love to make sense of things and turn chaos into order. They are dedicated, hardworking, and never stop until the job is done, and done right!

On the flip side, many people are annoyed by Virgos' can-do spirit. They can be anal-retentive and controlling. Anyone who's married to a Virgo, as I am, has spent much of their life searching the house for the things the Virgo has "put away" or "put in the right place." Needless to say, this can be a frustrating trait. When a Virgo is not balanced, they can be overly analytical and harsh in their judgments, even toward themselves. They can obsess over the tiniest detail. Until the problem is solved, the Virgo mind will not rest—they drive those around them bonkers!

The soul lesson of a Virgo is to understand that he or she does not have to strive for perfection, since everything in the universe is already in perfect order. Virgos also need to learn how to stop enabling others: No one learns by being enabled. (A caterpillar needs no help in transforming into a butterfly; nature has already taken care of this miraculous feat.) Virgos need to step back and let The Divine do His work. As much as they may like to believe so, Virgos are not God. They are only distracting themselves from their own missions as they try to act as God to the world around them. A Virgo who finally understands that everything is as it should be, in perfect divine order, can only then ascend to the greater light.

Famous Virgos include Warren Buffett, Prince Harry, Michael Jackson, Sean Connery, and Lyndon B. Johnson.

Libra (born September 23–October 22): Libra is the seventh sign of the zodiac and an air sign. The symbol of Libra is the scales of justice. It is always shown with the weight evenly distributed, keeping everything in perfect balance. Libras are always seeking harmony and peace, which means they sometimes avoid conflict that needs to be addressed. And though they can see both sides to every situation, they are not good with confrontation and might fail to point out both sides if it means they have to be confrontational. When my cousins, brothers, and sister and I had arguments about what game to play or where to set up the lemonade stand, my sister Susan, the Libra, always figured things out and settled them for us.

Libras have a high level of intuition and are the psychic sponges of the zodiac. They are extreme empaths, being susceptible of the feelings, thoughts, and emotions of others. No words need to be spoken around a Libra, since they can assess the energy around them on a subconscious level. When they can't find peace, Libras become unraveled and can turn angry, lashing out at others. Another negative trait is that because they can see both sides, they often have a hard time committing to one thing or another. They are especially wary of things that are long-lasting, because they imagine all the alternate possibilities that are shut down with each choice. Sometimes, Libras will conjure up excuses as they try to convince themselves that they shouldn't take on certain responsibilities. In the long run, they are only fooling themselves.

The soul lesson of a Libra is to find peace in each decision and let go of the past. Libras need to shut down their logical mind at times and listen to what their soul is trying to tell them. Accepting what is, rather than what should be, is a huge lesson for the Libra. Libras will understand themselves better when they learn how to stay in their own lane and allow conflicts around them to work out, rather than taking one for their team by making concessions for the sake of keeping the peace. If they learn to let go and let God handle it, life for the Libra will finally make sense.

Famous Libras include Julie Andrews, Simon Cowell, Judge Judy, Barbara Walters, and Mahatma Gandhi.

Scorpio (born October 23–November 21): Scorpio is a water sign and is the eighth sign of the zodiac. Scorpio's symbol is a scorpion with its highly venomous stinger. Scorpios are self-sufficient, giving, and passionate and can be loads of fun. They are very charismatic and know who they are. If they trust you, they are loyal to a fault. Scorpios are the ones who will do business with a handshake. When a Scorpio gives you their word, they honor it. My bestie Camille is a Scorpio and her word is her badge of honor. The physical attribute of any Scorpio I have ever known is their incredible, piercing eyes. Oh, Camille's eyes? They are a beautiful seafoam blue. But those eyes don't give much away; it's hard to know what they are truly thinking. Don't play poker with a Scorpio!

Similar to a scorpion, which has a deadly sting, Scorpios can be a little cagey and threatening. They don't trust easily and tend to put up their guard when in the company of a stranger. If you give them time, however, you'll see that they are sensitive creatures who are highly intuitive. Power-hungry Pluto rules Scorpio, so they are often driven by power as they seek positions of authority and the almighty dollar.

One attribute that can slow down a Scorpio on their spiritual journey is that they can be extremely jealous and possessive, and their need to control people and situations often leads to failing relationships. Also, they hate to be perceived as weak, so they are hesitant to reveal their vulnerabilities. The Scorpio's soul lesson is to give up the inner battle between darkness and light. The death of the ego can be Scorpio's biggest salvation. Once Scorpios learn to use their power with love and compassion, and not just for the sake of power, they can tear down the walls that have imprisoned them and experience true spiritual freedom.

Famous Scorpios include Bill Gates, Martin Scorsese, Ivanka Trump, Theodore Roosevelt, Hillary Clinton.

Sagittarius (born November 22–December 21): Sagittarius is the ninth sign of the zodiac, a fire sign. The symbol for Sagittarius is an archer pointing an arrow up to the heavens. Sagittarians aim high—toward gaining wisdom and finding the true meaning of life. The ruling planet of Sagittarius is Jupiter. Jupiter is the largest planet of the solar system—the planet of expansion. Sags continually expand their viewpoints through their intense curiosity and philosophical minds. They are the world travelers of the zodiac, and no matter where life takes them, it is very easy for them to call that place home. My niece Maria, who's in her early 30s, has already traveled to 47 countries. She's a new mother, with new responsibilities, but her passport is still getting as many stamps on it each year as before she gave birth. Nothing can keep her from quenching her thirst for new knowledge and new, exciting adventures.

Not only do Sags like to learn new things, they like to teach others what they've learned. It's great to have a Sag in your life because they are the happiest people in the zodiac. With their loving, carefree approach to life, they don't sweat the small stuff. Sags seem to have more faith in The Universe than the average Joe; balanced Sags typically are not ruled by fear and influence those around them to embrace adventure and reject fear as well. Sags value freedom over anything; they'll turn down a high-paying job if it means they'll have to give up their freedom. That love of freedom is a love of spontaneity as well, which isn't a bad trait unless you need them to stick to a particular plan.

On the negative side, the ever-honest Sag will often offer their unsolicited opinion, which can be a little hard to take. And if you dish it back to them, they get their feelings hurt. They can be very opinionated in a debate and sometimes get a little aggressive in order to "win." They don't like to hang around people who challenge their beliefs or who disagree with their lifestyle. This is why family gatherings can be short-lived for the Sag who likes to be in their own private oasis.

A Sag's soul lesson can be a bit challenging: They often see commitment as something that will restrict or stifle them in their quest to find their truth. What Sags need to learn is faith, and a commitment to faith. Sags need to trust the soul over their own impulses, so they can see that they are no different from Dorothy in *The Wizard of Oz*, who went on a big adventure to another land only to find that true freedom, her home, was in her heart.

Famous Sagittarians include Frank Sinatra, Steven Spielberg, Brad Pitt, Britney Spears, and Mark Twain.

Capricorn (born December 22–January 19): Capricorn is an Earth sign and is the tenth sign of the zodiac. The symbol for Capricorn is a sea goat—the head of a mountain goat with the tail of a fish. Yeah, I've never seen one in real life either. In my opinion, this symbol when simplified looks like the letters *V–S* written in script. Those born under this sign are usually workaholics who are motivated and ambitious. Capricorns dig their hooves into the ground and just keep going. Capricorn's ruling planet is Saturn, the disciplinarian of the zodiac. If you're having a yard sale, I recommend asking a Capricorn to lend a hand. They will not only drag the dusty items down from your attic and out of the garage, but they'll clean up and arrange them on the lawn so it looks like an auction at Sotheby's. Oh, and don't worry, they won't leave your side until every last item is sold.

Honest, reliable, and sensible, Capricorns are people pleasers. On the negative side, Capricorns have trust issues and can become distant and cold when they're not feeling safe with you. Their emotions run deep and they usually aren't willing to share them. You might find yourself playing a guessing game if you have a Capricorn mad at you: "Did I do this? Did I do that? What did I do?!" Since they're very goal-oriented, they often do not have time for small talk and will politely excuse themselves to get down to business. Their constantly spinning minds can make them inaccessible to the rest of us.

The soul lesson for a Capricorn is to understand what is truly important in life before it's too late. Capricorns need to learn to stop and smell the flowers. In their perpetual race to please everyone around them, they are frequently depleted, exhausted. Capricorns need to treat themselves the same way they would treat a child who needs unconditional love and compassion. They need to understand that they are just as good as anyone else. Once they see life and themselves through the eyes of The Divine, they will finally experience true love—a love that can never be attained through hard work or by pleasing others.

Famous Capricorns include Elvis Presley, Muhammad Ali, Tiger Woods, Kate Middleton, and Michelle Obama.

Aquarius (born January 20–February 18): Aquarius is the 11th sign of the zodiac. The symbol for Aquarius is a woman holding an urn, pouring water. This is usually depicted by two wavy lines, one atop the other. Aquarius is an air sign, ruled by the planet Uranus (Uranus controls the airwaves), so most modern-day astrologers say those wavy lines represent electrical waves and not water. Aquarians are humanitarians to the core; they are the do-gooders of the zodiac who dream of changing the world. If you have an Aquarian pal, surely they've talked you into joining whatever do-good mission they're on lately. They are social butterflies who have many friends, but they are ultimately more interested in the quality of their relationships rather than quantity.

If they're not saving the world at large, Aquarians are helping to bring about change in their own world. They have great intelligence and a knack for technology, and they are content inside their own heads. They're so content, in fact, that it's sometimes hard for them to join the rest of us in the real world. If you're looking for someone to express emotion, don't look toward an Aquarius. Like the spontaneous Sagittarians, Aquarians also value their freedom. However, they aren't necessarily seeking physical freedom; instead, it's the freedom to think without the influence of others. They can be eccentric and erratic, but that's the stuff that geniuses are made of.

On the negative side, these smarty-pants can get pretty angry. They'll overthink things and won't listen to reason once they've made up their mind about something. When out of balance, they can be erratic and dogmatic, or even worse, wickedly sarcastic and utterly rebellious. If you cross an Aquarian, they'll cut you out of their life and never speak to you again. If you're in a relationship with one of these geniuses, you're better off expecting the unexpected than waiting for anything in particular. The soul lesson for an Aquarian is to open up their emotional side in order to experience compassion, gratitude, and love. The Aquarian needs to embrace his divine nature, along with the divinity of others, which is the ultimate goal of every soul.

Famous Aquarians include Thomas Edison, Bob Marley, Ellen DeGeneres, Rosa Parks, and Oprah Winfrey.

Pisces (born February 19–March 20): Pisces is the twelfth sign of the zodiac and is a water sign. It is represented by two fish swimming in opposite directions connected by a cord. Pisces are like that—always swimming in two directions at once. They cannot stay put! Some people call it attention deficit disorder; I call it sun in Pisces. If you want to have fun, spend the day with a Pisces. They live in a continuous state of compassion, and like water, they flow into and fill all the people around them. The downside of this is that they feel everyone else's emotions along with their own and often have a hard time differentiating between the two. On most days, Pisces are connected to the spiritual realm more than the physical. They need to be reminded to come down to Earth and stay grounded. Their spiritual influences put them in creative roles, like writers, musicians, and inventors. They receive inspiration from above as well as from the world around them and put this inspiration to good use in their creative pursuits.

On the negative side, Pisces can be too sensitive for their own good. Many Pisces suffer from addiction problems, since their overly empathic reality can be too hard to manage, resulting in a continual search for escape routes. They are idealistic, so they are frequently disappointed. Some people call them Debbie Downers. Since the nature of a Pisces is duality, they need to find a way to bring balance between the higher realms of the spiritual world and the lower realms of the three-dimensional world. It would be wise for airy-flighty Pisces to put a bumper sticker on their car, or a magnet on their fridge, to remind them that they are not humans having a spiritual experience, but rather spiritual beings having a human experience. Simply put, they need to better integrate peace and love from the heavens into their three-dimensional world. They need to have that human experience.

Famous Pisces include Albert Einstein, Justin Bieber, Steve Jobs, Jessica Biel, and Carrie Underwood.

Each one of us has a unique personality. These personalities have different aspects that are magnified or suppressed according to our zodiac. When we hide our true nature, when we fight against what pulses naturally from within us, that is when conflict arises in our lives. But when we understand the placements of the planets and stars, and how that placement influenced us at birth and continues to influence us today, then we can tune ourselves in to who we really are. And to be our genuine, authentic selves, exactly as God made us, is the only way to find our soul purpose.

SATURN RETURNS

Although each planet has a role, Saturn is the one you should know as you search for your soul purpose. You can learn more about Saturn, or *Saturn Return*, in books at the library or on the internet. But I'll give you a quick overview, so you can see how this feisty old orb has been working in your life thus far. I say *feisty* because Saturn can take a joke—though, when it comes to teaching lessons, he's all business.

When you were born, Saturn was located in a particular part in the sky, a particular place in your personal birth chart, or horoscope wheel. From the moment of your birth, Saturn begins to slowly work its way back around the wheel of the sky. It takes 27 to 30 years for it to return to the exact place it was at your birth. This is known as the Saturn Return. Until you have your first Saturn Return, you are living out karma from your past lives. Whether they were good lives or bad, your soul has the answer and knows what needs to be done. The good news is, if you hate your life up to 29, you can now look forward to better opportunities. Your karmic debt has been paid and you can move on to better choices that will help elevate your soul.

During your early life, Saturn sort of takes a back seat. I can picture him sitting back, legs kicked up on the desk, with his arms up behind his head, waiting for you to get on with the show. He understands that you first must let go of the past and hit a certain level of maturity before he springs into action to help out. This is when Saturn offers his first wake-up call. It's like a screeching fire alarm that goes off when you least expect it—*BOOM*—Saturn makes his grand entrance. He shows up, investigates the damage you've done, and then lays down the law. And you darn-well better listen!

When I had my first astrological reading, I was shocked to learn about Saturn's role in our lives. If we are the children of the zodiac, Saturn is our parent. And like a strict parent who wants to impart all their wisdom, much discipline is brought into play. Saturn is the parent who gives his children tough love to see positive results. And, as any good parent would do, he is always making his rounds to ensure that his kids stay on track to finish their chores. Saturn can be tough, but he plays fair. When he's not acting as a parent, he's acting as trainer at the gym, pushing you to pump more, lift more, kick more, until you've gone beyond your limits. He knows how far you can go and he'll scream at you until you get there. When the results come in, he's just as happy as you.

Essentially, though Saturn acts as our teacher and our trainer, his job is to make us see that we are smarter than we think and stronger than we think. We have what it takes to pull through. He also reminds us that there are no shortcuts in achieving our goals; the only way to achieve positive results is through our own hard work, dedication, and perseverance. Saturn is a stickler about who we allow to help us on our journey—not just any Joe will do! Saturn's methods may be harsh, but they sure prove to be productive.

Once Saturn has returned, the structure of your life is subject to change, since Saturn is now in charge. Do you go back to school for an advanced degree? Do you change your career? Move out of your parent's home? Marry the love of your life? Or buy your first home? All of these life-changing questions propel you into the next phase of your life. Saturn is the force that gets you on the path that your soul chose prior to your birth. You may have forgotten why you came, but Saturn has it all stored in his memory bank.

The second time Saturn returns to your natal position is around the ages of 57 to 60. Again, as you enter this phase, questions of retirement, downsizing, or even traveling to places you've always dreamed of arise. Finding fulfillment in your life can loom large. Saturn forces us to look at and answer important questions, such as: Am I living my purpose? What is my purpose? Did I follow my dreams and is there still time to do so? No matter where you are on your journey, Saturn can always be found, in one part of your astro chart, giving you the reminders and discipline necessary for soul growth.

There's no quiz in this chapter—let's pretend it's Spring Break. But wait! There is homework, and that is to find your astrological combination (including your sun, moon, and rising sign). Then look back in your life and see if you can figure out when Saturn returned and when he's due next.

11

Rising Above It All:
Ascending to New Spiritual Heights

> *"Ascension is the triumph of mastered emotions;*
> *a process of gaining clarity in the darkness of*
> *blind spots and struggles, allowing you to*
> *perceive with the karmic intelligence of the Soul."*
>
> —KA CHINERY

WHAT I am about to tell you in this chapter may be old news to some of you—though, to many of you, this news will be shocking. Either way, pay close attention. As you read on, try to absorb the information through the center of your heart chakra. That is, don't just take these words in the way you might download a file onto your computer: *click, click, click, drag to file*. Instead, allow this information to resonate through your Highest Self, your most knowing Self, your God-connected Self.

My purpose in writing this book has always been to help you find your soul purpose during this lifetime. What I haven't told you yet, and what I would be remiss to omit, is that your greatest soul purpose might be to simply *be here now*. To have been born in this age means you agreed to be a part of a massive paradigm shift taking place throughout our planetary system. In our current evolution, we are raising the collective consciousness of The Universe. This shift in consciousness is called the ascension process. Follow along with me as I explain this in further detail.

Being alive in a three-dimensional body today is like watching the greatest show on Earth. Or maybe I should say, the greatest show in the universe. I'm sure you're asking why. *Why is now different from any other time in history?* I'll tell you why! Most people fear what they don't understand. So I'll try—as I have tried throughout this book—to deliver the information in the most gentle and loving way.

To make it simpler, let's backtrack for a minute. If you read my first book, *The Happy Medium: Life Lessons from the Other Side*, you know the story of how I stumbled into my husband Anthony's spirit guide, Kali, by accident. (Well, not really by accident. Anyone who's read this far knows there are no accidents, only occurrences that our three-dimensional minds read as accidents.) Here's what happened, in brief. I had gone to my local library and checked out a book that had step-by-step directions for how to conduct a "past life" regression. Past life regression therapy is the act of bringing forth your soul's memories of experiences you had in past lives. In doing this, we can recognize and examine the emotional baggage we've carried with us from other lives so we can better understand why we act and think the way we do in this life.

Anthony, my stable Virgo husband, agreed to be my guinea pig as I taught myself how to do this. Either my library book happened to show the best, A-plus way to do past life regression therapy, or Anthony just happened to be the perfect person on which to execute my little experiment. Or, most likely, it was a combination of both. In any event, in our comfortable living room in Long Island, I hypnotized Anthony with absolutely no problem. You can imagine how surprised I was when he started to speak to me under hypnosis. The first thing he said was, "Kali's here." After that, it wasn't Anthony speaking, it was Kali herself, who, she explained, was using Anthony's vocal cords and mouth to communicate with me.

Kali proceeded to tell me that she was Anthony's spirit guide and has been with him since his birth. You can be sure that the first few questions I asked Kali were deliberately tricky so that I could be sure it wasn't an evil spirit who wanted to manipulate me. I won't go over which questions I asked, but believe me, I tested Kali in every direction. No matter what I dished out, Kali passed with flying colors.

Kali told me that she has never been apart from Anthony since he came into his current body. When he was a little boy who was terrified of being alone in his dark bedroom on the top floor of his house, Kali stayed with him. When Anthony was nine years old, he climbed 30 feet up a schoolyard tree. Of course, being the restless kid he was, it didn't take much for Anthony to fall off a branch and start plummeting to the ground. Was he hurt? No! Kali was there, manipulating his fall so that he was slowed as he bounced off many other branches on the way down. When he hit the ground, the teachers couldn't believe that Anthony didn't even have a scratch. As I've said before, my husband is my rock: solid, dependable, level-headed. But as a kid, he was hyper and wild. Kali had her work cut out for her with Anthony in keeping him on the right path. She even helped him avoid a deadly car accident in his early teens.

I like to think of Kali as someone like Genie in the Disney movie *Aladdin*. (Though I'm pretty sure Kali can't grant all of Anthony's wishes. And I doubt she has the song and dance skills Genie shows off in the film in numbers like *Friend Like Me*.) Unlike Genie, Kali doesn't throw gold coins down on Anthony. Instead, she stands on the sidelines and waits for him to ask for her help, which he does pretty regularly. Of course, until that day when I hypnotized him, Anthony didn't realize that every time he'd called out for help in the past—when he was scared or in danger—he was calling out to Kali. Now he knows that Kali is standing near him ready to jump in and help, and he's very grateful to her.

Since that day, I have put Anthony under hypnosis many times and have had numerous conversations with Kali. Kali and I have bonded in many ways and, like true friends, I put my full trust in her and all the wisdom she has to pass on. Kali and I usually talk about the spirit world and The Universe, but she also likes to remind me of the many, many times she sprang into action to save Anthony's butt.

While Anthony has Kali, I have a spirit guide named Malick (short for Malachi, a name I heard during my Christian upbringing). Malick talks to me the way other spirits do: I descramble the incoming signals into thoughts and words that make sense to me. I've grown used to Malick, and I trust him and all the messages he sends me.

During a recent hypnosis session with Anthony, I was confused and surprised when a new spirit guide stepped forward to speak to me through Anthony's vocal cords and mouth. He announced himself as Tuzeu, pronounced *Too-Zoo*. He didn't tell me how to spell it, so I decided to spell it this way. Tuzeu told me that he was an assistant to Malick. Malick has sent other spirits to speak with me before, but they were never called assistants. I asked Tuzeu where Malick was. Tuzeu said that Malick was busy helping others and that I could rest assured that he (Tuzeu) would take good care of me as Malick's surrogate. Surrogate? Really?! Tuzeu was going to be my Malick? The idea of a surrogate did not sit well with me. I grilled Tuzeu, just as I had grilled Kali the first time I met her. Actually, I was harder on him than I was on Kali. I put Tuzeu through the paces until his answers and my intuition determined that he was 100 percent authentic.

Remember, intuition is a great resource when you're looking for the truth or trying to decide if someone is authentic or real. I encourage you to use yours as much as possible—your intuition is your God-given human barometer. I'm sure you've heard the expressions "trust your gut" and "I have a gut feeling." These are apt expressions: Your gut really is where God talks to you through intuition.

Tuzeu explained that Malick was very busy. It turns out that Malick has great power and control in the spirit realm. (Yes, there's a ranking in the ether, just as we are ranked here in the three-dimensional world.) I asked if Malick was ranked higher than Kali. Tuzeu said, "Oh, yes! Malick oversees many souls on Earth and is the boss of many other spirit guides." Of course, I prodded and poked. I wanted to know what kind of boss Malick was—the one who pals around with you cracking jokes, or the one whose presence in the room makes everyone else silent? Well, it turns out he's more like the latter. Souls in the spirit world fear Malick, Tuzeu told me. What Malick wants, Malick gets. This was shocking to me. In my eyes, Malick was an all-good, benevolent guide who looked over me and helped me in every way possible. Was Malick a mean spirit? I wondered.

I was relieved when Tuzeu explained that Malick was far from mean-spirited. (It's funny how we use the word *mean-spirited* to describe living people, when it's much more applicable to the spirit world.) In fact, Malick is the opposite of mean-spirited! It was Malick's unconditional love and understanding of others that led him to his position as a high-ranking guide. "Maybe *fear* was the wrong word," Tuzeu said. Yeah, it sure was! If you tell me people "fear" someone, I think it's because they're mean or scary—you probably think that too. Well, we're both wrong. Tuzeu explained that often we fear the people we most respect because we feel that we may fail in comparison to them. This is the case with Malick. Few spirits feel they can keep up with him.

Yes, even when we've left our physical bodies and exist as balls of energy, we can live in fear. In many episodes of my television show *The Haunting Of . . .* I met spirits who carried strong emotions, including fear, which we'd expect people to leave behind after exiting their three-dimensional existence. Thankfully, in time, their own angels and spirit guides help them to move closer to the light where love banishes all fear.

I have to admit, I felt special knowing that I had such a wise, high-ranking guide. I made it a point to ask Tuzeu why some people have higher-ranked guides than others. I mean, why would Anthony, my rock of a husband, have a spirit guide who was ranked below my guide? Tuzeu made the answer sound so simple, I was surprised I hadn't just seen it myself.

Our Earthly missions we agree to with God vary from person to person. The bigger our mission on Earth, the higher ranked the guide who's sent to watch over us. This made me wonder about the ranking system. How did I know Malick was qualified to be my guide? Who achieves what rank, and how? Was there a panel of judges from different countries, as in the ice-skating competition in the Olympics? Tuzeu explained that all guides are souls who once lived in our three-dimensional world, and their ranking is based on how many lives and lessons the soul has experienced. The highly advanced guides like Malick are ones who have been around the block so many times, they understand the inner workings of the soul and how to navigate the three-dimensional world.

Tuzeu compared the spirit hierarchy to a school district. Some guides are like teachers in the school: They've had special training to get where they are and to teach their specialized subject. Tuzeu added, "Kim, you wouldn't find a kindergarten teacher teaching college courses, right?" A lightbulb lit up in my head—I was starting to get it. Tuzeu went on with his school metaphor. Each department has a department head or chair, and that person is more experienced in school systems than the teachers; he or she's been around longer. Above them all is the principal of the school—someone who's done all the jobs below him. And above the principal is the superintendent. This person has been through all parts of the school system and understands each part so well that he acts as the CEO of the district. He manages the entire mass of people, so they can better work in their specific domains. It turns out Malick is like the superintendent of schools. He's a very busy guide who is getting so much done for The Universe.

As I listened to Tuzeu speaking, I wanted to run out into the street and tell all the world about the spirit world and how it works. I wanted to tell the whole world they are not alone—far from it, in fact: We are all connected by the great force of God, the great force of love. And I wanted the world to know that death is not the end, it is only part of the process. In fact, we never die! The only thing that vanishes is our bodies. You've heard the phrase "ashes to ashes, dust to dust." We start as nothing of substance, ashes, and return to nothing of substance, dust. And still *we exist!* We, our souls, continue cycling through one dimension into the next and back again. Before I could stop myself, the following words spilled out of my mouth: "Tuzeu, would you like to help me write my next book?"

Tuzeu laughed. And then he said, "I'll have to check with Malick on that." At first, I thought he was joking. But then I could hear the seriousness in his (Anthony's) voice.

Once I put my mind to something, nothing will stop me. I knew I couldn't wait until Malick approved this project. The psychic journalist in me took advantage of the fact that I had Tuzeu's undivided attention. I asked him every question that was flooding into my mind. The first question was, "What should my next book be about?" He answered immediately with two simple words: *the soul.* Because spirits have a broader point of view and aren't living in linear Earth time, I figured a discussion had already taken place between Malick and Tuzeu about what the subject of my next book should be. In fact, they probably knew every chapter of this book before I even sat down to write it! I asked Tuzeu to tell me more—what was I to say about the soul?

Tuzeu answered me slowly and deliberately. I could tell that what he was saying was important and might change my life. And listen, if something's going to change my life, then I want it to change yours too!

The planet Earth, Tuzeu explained, is currently going through an enormous frequency shift: We are raising our collective electrical frequency. Also, mankind is evolving more rapidly than at any other time in human history. The increased unrest around the globe is forcing people to reexamine their lives and ask the most important question of all: *What is the true meaning of life?* Our souls, whether we're aware of it or not, are trying to push us toward lives of greater meaning. In moving forward, we are looking backward in many ways, back to our origins, our roots.

Great numbers of people are stumbling into forgotten and even hidden knowledge contained in the Mystery Schools, which have existed around the world since the beginning of mankind. Until now, the teachings of these Mystery Schools were kept under lock and key, with access only given to people with particular spiritual powers. Those who had the eyes and ears to hear the truth were granted access. The truth, which has always been understood by a small number of spiritualists, is now spreading to all those who seek it.

The word *truth* in the spiritual world means *God.* And by that I mean that there is nothing that is apart or separate from God. God is absolute. So in existing, in having consciousness, you have God and are a part of God. The Bible says, "The truth will set you free." Love is truth. God is love. Therefore, truth is God. When you are one with God you are truly free.

As I kept pestering Tuzeu with questions, he told me that we are reverting to the wisdom God gave us—wisdom that has long been forgotten. We are implementing ancient knowledge that is already deep within us and can be accessed if we release from our minds all the lies that our egos have taught us. When we dig deeper into this wisdom, we will find our way back to ourselves, to our true divine nature. Ancient communities had easier access to this wisdom. They were closer to it and closer to God. Mankind survived for thousands of years on this wisdom alone. It was how we decided where to build shelter, how to deliver a baby, what to eat, and how to heal the sick. We used all the elements of the Earth, all the powers of the Earth, all that God gave us when we were created. We knew everything we needed to know: how to love, give, and exist in the spiritual world. Sadly, today, this wisdom is often obscured by the quest for material goods, along with our massive egos and vanity.

Tuzeu reminded me that there have been people throughout history who transcended the limitations of the physical world. If you look back through time you will find spiritualists who could levitate off the ground. And there have been many people who could walk through walls, sleep on a bed of nails, or walk barefoot across hot coals. Tuzeu said, "It is no secret that as the Earth becomes filled with more light strands from the higher dimensional frequencies, humanity is being transformed. People are being tapped on the shoulder and reminded to wake up from their spiritual slumber." And because Tuzeu can talk a mile a minute without interruption, he went on to say, "Since the Earth is raising her vibrational frequency, so too must everything with a vibration rise up, including humans. Our galaxy is vast and wide, and what affects one planet will have an impact on surrounding planetary systems." In other words, we are in the midst of a collaborative effort to elevate the frequency (vibrations) of ourselves and the universe.

So what does this mean? What is happening now? Believe me, I had the same questions you have.

What this means is that we are evolving toward a life where we live through our heart chakras rather than through our lower chakras. This higher mindset is closer to God and connected to higher dimensions. Within this mindset the death of the ego is imminent. The ego operates out of the lower chakras and is connected to the mental matrix of the currently programmed three-dimensional world. I would love to write a whole book explaining the mental matrix of our current modern world. And maybe one day I will. But for now, and for the purposes of this book, I'll explain the Matrix in brief.

One of my favorite films is *The Matrix*. If you haven't seen it yet, I recommend you do. *The Matrix* is science fiction, though I think it perfectly reflects the current state of humanity on Earth. In *The Matrix*, the human race is put into a hypnotic state, or essentially put to sleep throughout their entire lives. What they think are their lives are actually a computer-generated simulation—an illusion that they think is reality. They experience everything as we do—they work, eat, sleep, drive cars, buy homes. But none of that is really happening, true reality exists outside their illusions. During the movie, a few characters realize what is happening and are able to break free of the Matrix, to transcend it into what is truly real.

Most of us today are living in a form of the Matrix: We are sleeping through what really matters and fully buying into the false world that surrounds us. The world we *think* matters is one driven by greed, money, material goods, sex appeal, and youth culture. But none of these things are connected to God. Living in this way is like being someone from an Eastern Bloc country who travels to the United States and tries to make purchases at Target with Russian rubles or Kazakhstani tenge. The checker won't take either—those currencies have no value outside their countries, just as our Earth-ungrounded egos have no value in the truth or to God.

Like the people in the movie who break free of the Matrix, we, too, need to break free of the ego-based, lower-chakra-driven life. Love, or God, is all there is and all that matters. Buying a new car and getting Botox (I've done one of those things and have considered the other!) are Matrix dream values. We think they'll help us, but that's just an illusion. We think they'll build interesting lives for us, but that's just a dream. In the movie, a character is handed a red pill that permits him to break away from the Matrix, allowing him to finally see clearly into a new reality, into the truth. For humans living in the consumer-driven, media-created Matrix, there is no red pill. But there is something we all have and can use: love and compassion. When love and compassion radiate straight from your heart chakra, a trapdoor is opened and you drop straight out of the Matrix and into the truth. And remember what truth is? Truth is everything that ego is not. Truth is God. Truth is love. God is love.

Tuzeu explained that humanity is in the process of rising above the dense, dark energies (the lower chakras) that we have been so conditioned to accept. For many years we have been buying into this darkness so readily that we don't even see it. But all that is changing. We are waking up and seeing it. We are carrying torches and illuminating the path, and we are changing the world.

As I mentioned in an earlier chapter, we are communal people who tend to follow the traditions of our community. These traditions hand us our religion, our holidays, how we raise our kids, how we dress, where we live, and how we spend money. Your community is your vibe and everyone should find the right community, with the highest vibrations. But there is a version of community culture that doesn't serve the soul, and that is when you follow the customs of your group without questioning them. To blindly follow what has been handed to you turns you into a mindless creature. It's another form of the Matrix. Make your choices with your eyes open, so that what you do, and who you bond with, represents your heart chakra and God—*not* Matrix-minded empty customs that we were taught to value.

Of course, we all have many happy moments in our families of origin when we are following rules and customs we never questioned. But true happiness comes when we break free of the rules that were created to separate people and magnify their differences. True happiness comes when we can drop the community habits of judgment and "otherness"; when we see others with love and compassion; when we see others as just like us in their connection to God.

One reason we so easily fall into the Matrix is fear. When we are consumed by fear, we ignore hidden truths that we know to be true. Like psychic sponges, we sop up all the energy of the collective ego-based mindset, leaving us feeling helpless, hopeless, and detached from our place of love: the heart chakra. Every day, we witness individuals and families being celebrated across every medium for their insatiable consumerism and greed, their focus on the three-dimensional body they happen to be in. This makes it very hard to resist the pull of the Matrix and the rules of the presumed authorities.

Fear leads us to believe the opposite of what is true: We live in a perfect universe, where there is a perfect solution to every problem, where every individual soul is perfect in its imperfections, and where there is no separation of any kind. You are me and I am you. In releasing thought patterns, fears, false authorities, and beliefs that do not serve the highest good, we open our heart chakras and turn our lives into a beautiful celebration filled with creativity, effortless joy, laughter, peace, and love.

This needs to be said again: We have to stop giving away our power to the presumed authorities. When we deny authority to these false leaders, we tap into the power and authority of The Universe that is contained within each of us. God is the only authority. God is love. We are love.

Tuzeu did not use the term *Matrix* when we spoke (I don't know if he was in a body when the movie came out) but he understood the gist of it. He said he wasn't concerned about the great number of souls currently living in an illusion-based reality, filled with darkness and lies. In a confident and matter-of-fact way, he told me that every soul would soon come out of their illusion. The Universe is sending out multiple wake-up calls, and one by one, each of us will receive this call. When you get the call, you will understand all the truth contained in your soul.

Things will change physically once you receive this wake-up call. Your spiritual vibrations will speed up. The vibrations of the world are increasing already. When our spirits catch up to the rapid vibrations of Mother Earth, each of us will feel the oneness with love and God. It's not easy to maintain a high vibration—they will fluctuate from day to day or week to week. Unless you've reached total enlightenment—like some of the great masters of our time—you have to float with the idea that you're simply aiming for the intention to continually maintain a high vibration. When the average frequency you maintain is high, you will be able to manifest all that you desire, whether it's positive or negative. I'll say it again as a reminder: The Universe does not discriminate. Remember the **Law of Polarity**? Here it is: The power to create what you want comes with the power to create what you don't want. You know the saying *Be careful what you wish for.*

To understand this better, picture yourself riding in a slow-moving car covered with rust and dents. The car is a body in the dense three-dimensional world. It is weighed down by the ideas of lack: *I want more, I want a nicer car, I want nice clothes, I want a bigger house.* Negative thoughts have power and weight. These ideas make the car dull, lacking all luster, and they slow it down.

Now imagine a bright red sports car, speeding past the slow, dull car. The sports car isn't weighed down with negativity and ideas of lack. This car has better ideas and proudly announces: *I am whole, I am abundant, I am love.* These thoughts are the weightless fuel that allows this car to zip down the road. And notice this car's brilliant, vibrant color. Lightness creates color, like the colorized world in *The Wizard of Oz.*

Be the sports car. When you have high-vibrating thoughts, it brings on high-vibrating action, which brings on more high-vibrating thoughts . . . It's a never-ending cycle that only increases in frequency and lightens as time goes on. Thoughts that connect you to God and The Universe are the highest-octane fuel you can get. Riding on that energy is like cruising an open road on a sunny day with the top down and your favorite music blasting. Weighing yourself down with nega-tive energy is like plodding along in traffic with black smoke puffing out your tailpipe.

Now, which car do you want to drive? What fuel do you want to use? The **Law of Attraction** gives you a choice, but the **Law of Vibration** yields the outcome. Live life with a high vibration and you'll be floating to your destination with music in your ears.

ONE FOR ALL AND ALL FOR ONE

When speaking of Divine Oneness, I must discuss the **Law of Polarity** again. As you read on, you will understand the importance of this law. Everything has its opposite: good and evil, black and white, hot and cold. For everything that exists, something counter to it also exists. The problem with duality occurs when it separates us, when we take a side. If your family practices a religion and you believe that religion is the only one to follow, you are enacting duality. You are saying, *The people who follow this religion are the best!* In doing this, you are sep-arating yourself from all the people who don't practice this religion. You are passing judgment; you are drawing a line and standing on one side of it. To live with this duality is not the way of God, or light, or The Divine. There is no duality in God. There is no duality in the spiritual realm. There is no duality in The Light and The Universe.

This does not mean you can't see both sides or see the duality. The two sides of a coin, the heads and tails, are very different; the images

are not alike at all. But you wouldn't say that one side of the coin is better than the other—you think of it as a whole coin, one thing. As it is
with a coin, so it is with life. The person who practices a religion might
be on one side of the coin, and the person who doesn't might be on
the other. But they are connected as one: They are both humans with
souls. They are one and the same.

A very dear friend Miguel came to the United States from El
Salvador with his wife, Carla. They were both in their early fifties when
they arrived and spoke very little English. Miguel and his wife are honest, humble, and hardworking people who appreciate every dollar they
have ever earned. Carla made some work connections through her
family, and quickly began cleaning houses. Miguel was lucky enough
to land a job working in a warehouse in Miami Beach. When orders
came in to the warehouse, it was Miguel's job to pull merchandise off
the shelves, pack it in boxes, get labels ready for shipping, and load the
heavy boxes onto the delivery trucks to be shipped out the next morning. Every day, Miguel started work at 6 a.m. and didn't leave the warehouse until every order was prepared for delivery. Some days he didn't
leave the warehouse until 8 p.m., only to get home, take a shower, eat a
quick dinner, and go to bed—waking up early the next day to do it all
over again.

Since Miguel's workweek was from Monday to Saturday, he only
had one day off to relax. Miguel was able to cope with the 90-degree
temperatures inside the warehouse during the winter months, but
during the summer the temperatures might rise to over 110 degrees. As
grateful as Miguel was to have a job with a weekly income, he couldn't
help but dread the thought of waking up day after day knowing he was
going to be working in a sweltering warehouse with no relief in sight.
To top it off, Miguel was not as young as the other men in the warehouse and had a few health concerns such as diabetes and arthritis.
With very erratic blood sugar levels, Miguel had to be extra-cautious
not to overheat to the point of exhaustion and dehydration. Arthritis
had already set in his knees, making Miguel move a bit slower than the
rest of the workers.

None of this was apparent to his boss or his coworkers, since
Miguel hid his pain well, and with a smile on his face always did what
he was told to do. Everyone who knew Miguel had nothing but good

things to say about him. Even though everything seemed to be working out well for Miguel, he couldn't get rid of the nagging thought that he didn't believe he could do this work much longer—it was taking too much of a toll on his health.

Carla knew her husband was doing more than he could handle. Some nights Miguel wouldn't even swallow the last bite of his dinner before he was passed out cold on the couch. Many evenings Carla didn't have the heart to wake him, so she would just cover Miguel with a blanket. Every day on his way to work, Miguel would tell himself, *I can't do this anymore and I don't want to do this anymore.* Some workdays were easier than others, and on those days his thoughts would alternate to *I'm grateful for this job and maybe it's not so bad.*

Miguel reminded himself every day that between his lack of education, his age, and his poor health, he had very few work options besides working at this hot and sweaty warehouse job. He felt stuck, but he had no other way to meet his monthly bills. Carla's job offered some financial relief, but the majority of her income had to be split with her boss. Miguel's warehouse manager heavily depended on Miguel and another young man to get all the orders out in time, and, as much as Miguel was pushing through long, hot days in the sweltering heat, nobody was the wiser to Miguel's health issues or to his nagging thoughts.

Whenever I saw Miguel I would ask him how everything was working out for him. His answer to me was always the same. With a big, brilliant smile he would answer me, "Very good—thank you, Ms. Kim: I am very blessed to wake up this morning and I thank God for giving me another day." I always wondered if he had been diagnosed with a deadly disease and was only given days to live, or if he was just very grateful to be alive for one more day.

One year had passed since Miguel started working at the warehouse and everything seemed to be going great, until one day I received a phone call from Carla. She apologized for calling me for help, but she didn't know what else to do: The warehouse manager decided to let Miguel go from his position. Through her tears, she said that both she and Miguel were confused about why he got fired. Miguel found termination papers in his locker, but his boss failed to give him a solid explanation of his reason for letting him go. As far as Miguel knew, his boss liked him a lot and was always expressing his gratitude toward Miguel for all his hard work. In fact, his boss always reminded him that he was the best worker the company had ever employed. He even gave Miguel advanced pay whenever he needed it and gave him the opportunity to work off the loan.

Carla thought I would have a clearer insight into why Miguel no longer had a job. When I asked my spirit guides to give me clarity on Miguel and his work situation, I immediately felt Miguel's heavy heart during his workweek, and I heard the thoughts he was thinking on a daily basis. I asked Carla if I could speak to Miguel to have him validate the information that I was receiving from my guides. Miguel came to the phone and I began relaying information that I was channeling.

Immediately I heard the words "Your wish is our command." Miguel did not quite understand this English expression, so I spelled it out for him. Based on the information I was receiving, I realized Miguel despised his job, and though he was a dependable employee who never missed a day of work, while projecting a happy vibe on most days, his thoughts of dread were creating a frequency that was broadcasting a very different story. Miguel admitted to me that every day he would play the lottery, hoping he would win so he could quit his job. He also admitted that he's a very proud man and it is his belief that it's his job, as a man, to provide for his wife and his family. He stated that he desperately wants to work, but he wishes he could get a job that was better suited for his health and his age.

Miguel couldn't resist asking me if I was able to psychically see him getting another job. I took a minute to tune in and then saw him driving a car with a person in the back seat. I asked him if he had a clean driving record and if he ever considered driving for a living. I told him that he could make his own hours while he drives around in an air-conditioned car taking people to their desired destinations. With excitement in his voice, Miguel proceeded to tell me that his brother-in-law drives an Uber cab and would often boast about how much money he makes for one day's work. Miguel said that he considered driving a car too, but he didn't want to leave the security of his warehouse job.

I explained to Miguel that since he wasn't proactive in leaving his job through his own decision making, The Universe did it for him, and because it understood his true vibrations, it responded accordingly.

Miguel's story perfectly demonstrates the **Law of Attraction** (vibrational thoughts aligning with physical manifestation), coupled with the **Law of Polarity.** What Miguel truly desired and needed was the opposite of his warehouse job, and his constant thoughts of needing a change catapulted him right into a new reality. I am happy to report that since The Universe orchestrated giving my friend Miguel a swift kick, firing him from his warehouse job, he has since decided to drive for Uber. Looking back, he understands how every one of his thoughts has connected to his current situation. I am so pleased to announce that Miguel is very happy and content in his current job.

The **Law of Polarity** states that in order to maintain the **Law of Balance** (keeping Miguel happy about his job), everything needs its opposite point (positive and negative). To understand the concept better, think of a simple battery that operates an electronic device. I'm sure you have seen the plus and minus signs (+ and −) inside the device where the batteries are inserted. The positive side of the battery has fewer electrons than the negative side, which holds a surplus of electrons. When positive and negative come together, it feeds the flow of energy perfectly, which is necessary to fire up the device. The same holds true for a magnet. When the electromagnetic fields align, there is a force that pulls them together. However, it must be understood that when this **Law of Polarity** is at work, even though both components have opposite attributes, they must work together to create the same desired outcome.

Returning to Miguel, everything about his job was negative, with hardly any positive thoughts present. To understand polarity better, it's helpful to use the analogy of the sun and the moon. They complement each other by creating light and darkness, or day and night. If the sun were shining 24/7, all our vegetation would dry out and die. In addition, if the sun never set, its light would halt our production of melatonin, which would signal our brains to stay awake. This process would interrupt our circadian rhythm (our body's internal clock), therefore creating a lack of sleep. Surely, this would be detrimental to the health of our planet, as well as to the health and well-being of the human species.

Tuzeu explained that all the Universal Laws work together to create a perfect universe—perfectly in sync and with perfect wisdom to remain constantly in a state of balance and harmony. I am so blessed to have received the wisdom of Tuzeu. I am blessed that he continues to meet with me to discuss higher wisdom.

During one of our more recent conversations Tuzeu asked me this question: "What experiences do you expect to have in your life?" I asked why he wanted to know. He answered, "Well, it's simple. The life you expect is the life you will get." The **Law of Attraction**! At that moment, I understood why Malick sent Tuzeu to me. I had already intuited that what Tuzeu had just said was true. We totally get each other—we vibrate on the same frequency! And though Tuzeu hasn't been with me for nearly as long as Malick, he is catching on pretty quickly to who I am. (Or maybe I'm catching on to who I am because of him. I guess it doesn't matter.) What does matter is that I like this dude. I like what he has to say. And, like him, I know that each day we're here on Earth we have the opportunity to live with our hearts pure and open, giving us the best day ever.

Part of my job is to zigzag across this great country and spread messages of love from the spirit world. My husband, Anthony, travels with me. Whether we are in a packed airport, jammed into a crowded plane, or sharing a hotel bathroom with all our toiletries shoved into one tiny bag, I always make sure to remind Anthony that we are on a great expedition. Every city, every hotel, every bus, train, cab, and subway we take is a new adventure with so much to explore. In embracing these adventures—in laughing over the pink shirt Anthony wore for four days straight when his luggage was lost—we are living in a love-filled, happy now.

Even if you don't travel at all, you can live an adventurous life. Adventure is a point of view, a way of experiencing life wherever you are at this moment. Great memories do not have to be built at historical sites, resorts, and tourist destinations. Nor do they have to revolve around proms, marriages, or 40th birthday parties. Great moments and great memories can happen in your office, at the deli, or as you push your grocery cart down the produce aisle.

So how do you do this? How do you make the here and now a beautiful adventure—no matter where that here and now is? How do you jump into the sports car, so you can feel like you're floating down the road instead of plodding along in the old, beat-up car? It's not hard. Remember, as Tuzeu said, "The life you expect is the life you will get."

Within you right this minute is the power to *change the energy* of most situations you may find yourself in. Here's a small exchange illustrating what I mean. Let's say the barista at your local Starbucks rolls her eyes when you shake your purse to gather the change in the corner. You could dislike her for that, or you could take yourself out of the equation and look at it from a greater distance. For all you know, she's been having a terrible day. Maybe she just got news that her mother has been diagnosed with a fatal illness. You don't need to know what happened to her before you place your order to see that her anger, frustration, or fear of *something other than you* is simply being vented on you.

This interaction is a chance for you to offer patience and kindness. You could hand over your change and say (with sincerity and no snark), "It seems like you're having a bad day. Is there something I can do to make it better for you?" I know many of you are shaking your head at the thought of extending a loving hand to a person who is lashing out at you. But trust me on this. It is hard, though not impossible, for someone to continue acting in anger and fear, when they are faced with a loving soul.

Sometimes simply offering to make it better opens a door for conversation and allows the other person to release their feelings without directing them at you. Sometimes it just makes people stop and think. It allows them to see themselves in the moment and in the broader context of the moment—to see that they are interacting with someone who has nothing to do with their problems. Of course, there are the stubborn few who want to hang on to their fear and anger, as if it's all they have to keep them afloat. Once you've opened your heart and offered it to them, there's nothing you can do but step aside and remove yourself from their energy.

I often wonder if some of my clients aren't necessarily coming to see me for an actual reading; rather, they're seeing me because they need someone to hear them out and to hear about their loved one who passed on. They want to be in contact with a person who will understand their pain. And they need to feel care, concern, love, and compassion from another being. Of course, when I give a reading, they are getting all that from me. Once their departed loved one has spoken and I have relayed their messages, I give my focused attention to the bereaved. There is often great relief and joy after they hear from their loved one who's passed on.

The spirits, it seems, offer those they leave behind everything they need to hear. It might not be exactly what the bereaved want to hear, but it is always what they need to hear. In getting that need met, a great relief floods in and the client usually exhales this relief with a flurry of words, stories, memories, and images they need to unload. Whether it's through a psychic reading, a therapy session, or a casual talk with family and friends, discussing your feelings can result in unloading the weight covering your heart, so that your heart can heal. By releasing negative emotions, which hijack your mind and your spirit, you are cleaning out the dirty energy and making space for clean, sparkling light to enter.

My conversations with Tuzeu have been very clear. He wants me to write about the soul. He wants the world to understand that light is what The God Force is made of, and this light is what will carry us home. Please understand that *home* is not a place, but a state of consciousness. It is the experience of Heaven, no matter where you are, even if you are still on the Earth. Tuzeu wants people in their three-dimensional bodies to activate their brightest, lightest bodies and their highest frequencies so they can graduate from the human condition to the spiritual realm—so they can ascend to the highest expression of God and all His love during this great cosmic shift.

There is a common idea circulating around spiritual communities that only the bravest souls have decided to come to Earth during this cosmic shift. If this is so, consider yourself one of the chosen. You are among the bravest and luckiest souls on Earth: You *are* the change the world has been waiting for. We are embarking on a great new cycle as we move from the Age of Pisces (the age of illusions, secrets, and lies) to the Age of Aquarius (the age of brotherly love, unity, and peace). Ideas about the Age of Aquarius have been swirling around our heads since 1969, when the 5th Dimension released the song *Aquarius (Let the Sunshine In)*. Though, really, ideas of peace and love have been trying to penetrate our souls from the moment we lost peace and love.

Congratulate yourself on being part of one of the biggest changes to come since the big bang: *the ascension.* The word *ascend* means to go up into the air, to rise, or to climb. Jesus died on the cross, came back three days later, walked the Earth for 40 days, and then ascended to Heaven. Like Jesus, we too—our souls, our truth—will ascend. But it's a little different from how it's described in the Bible.

The ascension process does not mean that you will be snatched up by aliens on a mysterious spaceship and dragged to Venus or Mars. In fact, it is not about going anywhere other than where you physically are right now. It is about achieving a higher state of consciousness. Whether you are in your shower at home, praying in temple or church, taking a deep breath while holding a difficult pose in yoga, or meditating on top of a rugged mountain—when you open your body to light and vibrate at a higher frequency, reality as you imagine it now will shift significantly. The ultimate mission of each of us is to transcend the solid, dense enclosure of our bodies. It is to leave the weighty ego-based and fear-based ways of the mind so that we can merge with the light and love of The God Force. Please understand that none of this is happening for us to escape from reality or to abandon humanity; in fact, just the opposite is true. We are being called to our higher purpose in order to salvage what is left of what God intended for our planet and all of its inhabitants.

Do you remember *Star Trek* (the TV show or the movies)? Remember the line, "Beam me up, Scotty!" This was the command that Captain Kirk gave to his engineer, Scotty, when he wanted to be transported back to the mother ship, *Starship Enterprise.* Being beamed was a mode of transportation, but often it was a way of saying, "Get me the heck outta this crazy place!" I'm sure that most of us have had a similar thought at some point in our lives. This desire isn't so far from your spiritual center. As souls, we are instinctively always reaching for God and trying to find our way back to our Source. Beaming, in fact, resembles the lightness of the soul and the soul's ability to ascend into the higher realm.

In order to beam up to God, in order to be released to join the higher consciousness (as Tuzeu tells me is happening now) we need to activate our light bodies. We need to unload all the baggage we're schlepping around and allow all the light of The Universe into our souls. Here are your directions for doing just that.

EMBRACE YOUR HEALTHY EGO AND
MOVE INTO YOUR SPIRITUAL BODY

I've mentioned the ego many times in this book. Really, I can't talk about it enough. The inflated ego is like the Devil, Hell, and your worst enemy all living right inside you. You do need an ego to survive on Earth. When you have a healthy ego, you can create healthy parameters and boundaries; you can love yourself enough to make sure that people treat you well and you treat yourself well. Also, a healthy ego can push you into survival mode. Though we don't need to hunt for our food, the ego helps us ensure that we have enough money or resources to eat a balanced diet (hopefully). Other than that, ego is the monster that takes over, forcing all your energy down into your lower chakras.

Some souls enter the three-dimensional world kicking and screaming. Still, we come because we know that the only way to evolve is by living in a harsh environment (Earth, surrounded by people) where feelings trigger our emotional body. These feelings bring to life our egoic mind, the exaggerated sense of self-importance, or importance in the wrong places. An egocentric life places values on things that don't matter: how you look, how much money you have, what car you drive, what your partner looks like, what kind of watch you wear, etc. It's almost like a director, set designer, and actor all rolled into one. It decides what "the audience," which is the world, will see. The ego then sets everything up *just so* and puts on a multidimensional show that has little to do with reality (the soul, The Divine) and only reflects the ego itself.

It is the ego's job to keep this show going at any cost. Many shows go way over budget. The bigger the budget, the bigger the ego, the bigger the illusion of greatness and superiority. And the bigger the show, the more energy it takes to keep it playing.

Have you ever attended a play and wondered how those actors can go up onstage night after night (sometimes for years) and speak the same lines over and over again? Well, if you've ever had an inflated ego (and all of us have at some point), you already know how exhausting it is. The ego wants to keep its show on Broadway for as long as possible. If you want to meet someone who is truly tired, find the person with the largest ego, the one who is putting on the biggest show. Sometimes the curtain drops, and the ego simply slinks off, totally depleted. This sounds like disappointment, but it's actually a good thing. When your ego leaves, you're left with your center, your truth, and your soul. The relief in returning to oneself, in being one's authentic self, is immense.

Unfortunately, though, the ego doesn't usually leave on its own. And it's hard for most of us to drop the story we've created about ourselves so that we can return to our authentic selves. We grow comfortable with our false identities and are scared of what we'd find when we release that identity. And then there's the basic problem of not even knowing *how* to drop the egocentric false self. When we realize that we need to embrace our true selves, I think it's best to remember that even the ego has a counterpart and presents a duality. The opposite of ego is humility. When we try to emulate the great ascended masters such as Jesus, Buddha, or Paramahansa Yogananda, we aim to leave our egos at the door and humbly walk the Earth. Still, we must accept what little ego lives inside us—the part that asks to be spoken to politely, that sets boundaries with people, and reminds us to bathe! We need to accept both sides of the coin of ourselves: ego and humility.

Here's more good news to help you maintain a healthy ego: The Universe is on your side and it knows that you need to fulfill your soul contract. And The Universe knows that your three-dimensional body is crammed full of ego and other false identities that block your soul's goals and weigh you down. That big Eye in the Sky is looking out for you and will create a scenario that will allow you to release all this dead weight. You've likely already received a few warnings and notices from The Universe. The warnings each of us get are different, but if you accept that God has His hand in everything, you'll be able to read the warnings He's sending you. My friend Joanne was fired from the retail job she hated, the job that kept her from pursuing her career as a dog trainer. That was the first big warning she got that she wasn't living her authentic life.

And if you miss the warnings, The Universe will put its foot down and insist, like a watchful parent, that you unload ego and fear so that you can unblock the barricades to your soul. When that foot comes down (Saturn is usually helping), things might not be pretty, but eventually they'll be better. Once your ego is kicked to the curb, your entire stage performance loses its luster.

Living with truth, with God, is easy. Living with falseness, with the ego, is hard.

When we let the ego go and live with the truth, we see the truth all around us. We see that we are one and the same, all of us connected to the same energy force and to God. This is where our community comes in. The ego will bond you with a community that reflects the ego. If we go back to our stage show metaphor, an egocentric life will pick a community that will promote the show, put up posters, buy billboards, and brag about the show on Facebook. The egocentric life will listen to false authorities in that community and might follow the rules of that community—rules that limit the soul but inflate the ego. A community that serves your ego is not a community that serves your soul purpose.

When you are living a soulful life, you can connect to like-minded people who support your soul and are reconnected to The God Force. If you connect with people who are soul-centered, as opposed to ego-centric, it can support you and keep you alive. Can an ant build an ant farm on its own? No! Can the queen bee build a hive and lay eggs on her own? Absolutely not! Can we exist alone? No—we never have and we never will: We are all a part of The Divine.

FORGIVE

Forgiveness is an important step in ascending to a higher conscious-ness. In order to become light filled, we must release energy that we no longer need. When we don't forgive, we are grasping onto anger and resentment. These emotions can play over and over in our minds, like a scratched 45 record on a turntable—with its needle stuck in one groove, repeating the same lyrics until we've internalized them as truth.

To forgive is to release past hurts and resentments. *This does not mean you are accepting or condoning the bad behavior of others.* You may have heard this expression: *Holding on to anger is like drinking poison and expecting the other person to die.* Most negative feelings, no matter who they're supposed to be directed at, turn in on us. That person you "hate," who you never see anymore, might have forgotten about you. They might be living a happy, productive life in another city. But if you're holding on to the anger you felt toward them, you are walking around with nothing but the weight and darkness of anger. You are poisoning yourself.

When we spew out negative emotions like anger, jealousy, and rage, we falsely think that we're bringing about change that will make us better. But what we're doing, in fact, is filling ourselves with negative emotions. When you yell at the driver who cut you off on the freeway, do you think she can hear? Do you think your words would change her life, or even just the way she drives? No, of course not. But you want to yell. Your ego wants to yell. And when you yell at your neighbor who ran over your mailbox, or snap at the barista who put regular milk in your coffee instead of almond milk, you are piling onto your soul-deadening, light-blocking emotions.

The human soul is like a giant water balloon. You can fill it and fill it and fill it, pumping water in. It will stretch and contort with all the water you put in, becoming a heavy, laden thing that won't float and bob. Instead, it sits on the ground until it's thrown and breaks apart, or until all that heavy water just bursts out with a sad, messy splat.

Anger, grudges, sadness, and fear overload your soul, block all the light, and keep you heavy, stuck here on Earth. You can't ascend to the higher vibrations with all that weight pinning you down. So what do you do? You release it all. And how do you do that?

You forgive.

Yes, forgive—everyone, and yourself.

If holding on to anger is like drinking the poison and hoping the other person will die, forgiveness is like pouring the poison down the drain and saving yourself and everyone else. When you forgive those who have done you wrong, you are admitting that you are complete and one with God, and that no one can really do you wrong. When you forgive yourself, you are accepting the perfection you were born with. You are honoring The Divine by honoring all the good that is inside you.

Forgiveness requires compassion. Think about what compassion is: shared suffering, motivated by a desire to alleviate the suffering of another. But to alleviate another person's pain, one must have empathy. Empathy is a step deeper than compassion: It requires synchronizing your emotion with another person's so that you actually feel their emotion. The ability to empathize begins in the first few years of life and develops through bonded social and emotional life events. To have empathy, one must first have their heart open to love. And by now, we all know what love is. That's right—love is the highest vibration there is: love is God. When you have compassion, you are admitting that we are all one and the same. When you feel empathy, you are connecting to that sameness. And empathy is not just what you feel when someone is sad or depressed. You also feel empathy for other people's happiness, joy, and even anger.

If someone is yelling at you, your first reaction is usually to get defensive. You take it personally. And in taking something personally, you put up a wall. Now, imagine their anger as a handball. When it hits your wall, it bounces right back to them, right? Does this solve anything? No. Your wall gets stronger, though more battered, and their anger multiplies and grows each time that ball bounces back. Someone in the midst of anger cannot feel empathy—cannot feel what you, the wall, are feeling. All they see is that handball slamming into the wall and bouncing back again.

The next time someone is yelling at you, try this: Mimic their body language. When you do this, when you adjust your body so that it mimes theirs, it will help you feel all their feelings. And when you feel their feelings, you stop being defensive, you tear down that wall against which they keep throwing the handball. The key to being able to do this is to take nothing personally. I know I've said it before, but it's worth saying again. Repeat after me: *Take nothing personally!*

Okay, back to the handball game. So you stand there and you mime the angry person and feel their feelings. What happens next? Well, their feelings no longer have a wall against which they can bounce back to their owner. So they float away, they dissipate. Next, just think *love*. Say the word over and over again. As the angry person's feelings float off, your love will float in. You and the angry person are one and the same. When you show empathy for this person, you are reminding him or her of that fact. You are connecting to them, rather than separating from them. You are creating unity instead of duality. The act of connection is an act of forgiveness. Anger divides—forgiveness unites.

Forgive and let the light in. A body and soul filled with light ascends and becomes part of the higher frequency.

I want to add one thing: Not only do you have to unpack emotional baggage through compassion and forgiveness, you must unpack physical baggage too. You are perfect. God does not make junk. So do not fill your body with junk. I'm talking about eating food made from chemicals, taking drugs, and ingesting any other substance that God did not intend for you to ingest. Even without knowing it, we are ingesting hundreds of toxins, maybe even thousands, that are being spewed into our environment from incinerators and fuel tanks, or taken into our bodies through cosmetics and air fresheners.

We need to continually detox both our minds of toxic thoughts and our bodies of toxic chemicals. As the greed of our world increases, I suspect the toxins all around us will increase too. Keep yourself as pure as you were the day you were born, and you will make yourself lighter still. You will be so light that nothing bad can hurt you; all will pass through you the way a bullet passes through air without harming it.

JUST BREATHE

If you've ever taken a yoga class, you've probably heard the teacher say something along the lines of "Do as much or as little as you can; the only thing required is that you breathe." Now, if you haven't taken a yoga class, you might think that sounds silly. But breathing is more than just inhaling and exhaling. Breathing is the basis of life. God gives us breath when we come out of the womb. Breath is what sustains us and keeps us calm. When we are in crisis, or in physical pain, the first thing we are told to do is to *just breathe.* There are even breathing techniques that are taught to women who are about to give birth. These techniques don't take away the pain of natural childbirth, but they help in making it more bearable.

When a person is stressed and reaches for a cigarette, they believe it is the cigarette that is calming them down. In fact, it is just the opposite. Nicotine is a stimulant. What calms the smoker down is the very act of breathing in deeply as they take a drag, and then breathing out slowly as they exhale the smoke. Breath is a gift that says, *Here you are, on Earth, in this body now.* When you breathe with deliberation, you are consciously enacting this gift and thanking God for it. You are connecting to your origins, to your original and authentic self, before ego and any emotional baggage entered the picture. You are going back to your pure, light self.

Meditative breathing quiets our minds, forces us into the moment, and connects us to a higher consciousness. Breathing, along with visualization or focusing on something beautiful, can help you release negative emotions that flow through the lower chakras, and fill you with lightness and air. This raises your frequency and floats your soul. Breathing is a way to activate ascension.

Here is a mantra you can use to bring sacred breath into your life as you release the poisons of fear and anger. I suggest you sit in a comfortable position, wearing comfortable clothes that allow your belly and your diaphragm to move in and out rhythmically. To further help you contain yourself in the pure light of a meditative moment, focus on an image of something beautiful that nature has created: a tree, a flower, grasses, the sun, the moon, or even a drawing of the Tree of Life. Now repeat this word in your mind over and over again: *So'ham.* Inhale as you say *so,* exhale as you say *ham* (rhymes with *mom* and not with *jam*). *So'ham* comes from Sanskrit and can be translated as *I am that.* That, of course, is everything. And everything is love. And love is . . . Yeah, I'll let you finish that sentence.

LAUGH IT OFF

Remember that scene in *Mary Poppins* when Mary, Bert, and the kids go and visit Uncle Albert? Uncle Albert is in the midst of a laugh attack and is floating on the ceiling. Bert quickly breaks down in laughter and then floats up to join Uncle Albert. Eventually, the kids also laugh their way up to the ceiling. By the end of the scene, Mary Poppins herself can't hold back and is floating on the ceiling with them, everyone buoyant and light with joy. It's a great moment in the movie, and one that aptly represents ascension.

Laughter can unblock your heart chakra to let in all the light of The Universe. This isn't something that's been made up to support the ideas of lightness and airiness. Doctors and sociologists have been studying the effects of laughter for decades. What they've found might astound you.

Laughter creates bonds. It unifies people. Often, laughter isn't about a response to something that's funny, it's an expression of joy. And when done in unity with just one other person or a group, it eliminates duality and creates a oneness. People often choose life partners who make them laugh; intuitively, they understand the union created through joined laughter.

Laughter relaxes you. When you laugh, your body releases tensions and the negative emotions that create those tensions. A good laugh can have the same effect as a massage.

Your immune system responds to laughter. Stress hormones decrease and immunity increases. You can laugh your way away from illness. If you're riding a crowded subway in the middle of winter with people coughing and sneezing all around you, just start laughing and your body will be more resistant to the germs around you.

Laughter is a pain reliever. Yes, you could take a Tylenol or Motrin. You could also laugh. Your body will release endorphins. Endorphins are the built-in painkillers that God gave you so that you wouldn't have to take a Tylenol!

Laughter is connected to the heart chakra. When you laugh, blood flow increases, arteries open up, and things flow as they should, thus protecting you from a heart attack.

Laughter eliminates negative emotions. It is impossible to maintain anger while laughing. And you can't feel stress or anxiety while you're laughing. You might feel them again the moment you stop. But laughing is an experience that can only happen when you are living in the present moment. And when you are in the present moment, those negative feelings have no validity. They are projections and reactions of the ego. Laughter is fully without ego.

The Universe wants you to laugh—that's why there are so many health benefits to doing it. When you tap into the joy of laughter, you will be lightening your load and allowing light to enter your soul. Who knows, maybe if you laugh long enough, you'll find yourself floating on the ceiling, just like Mary Poppins.

GIVE THANKS

Gratitude is another way to connect to God. Many people may not realize that giving thanks is an act of free will. Although it seems easy enough to give thanks, it is not that easy when life has handed us a raw deal. Staying in a state of gratitude when times are tough sends a message throughout the heavens that you are willing to have faith and stick it out until the end, when the blessings are ready to appear.

Gratitude changes our bodies, minds, and souls. It is a soothing salve that creates peace and calmness. Studies have shown that spending five minutes making a gratitude list will lower your blood pressure and increase your happiness. People sleep better and have less pain in their bodies after making gratitude lists. Depression has been shown to decrease by 35 percent simply by making a daily gratitude list. And people who dwell in gratitude have abundant energy and enthusiasm. Gratitude feeds your heart. In truth, it could save your life.

Gratitude connects us to higher-vibrating communities. Remember the spiritual **Law of Attraction**? When you are grateful, your vibrations rise, which then pulls in other high-vibrating people. Like attracts like. The more grateful you are, the more people you pull in; the faster their frequency vibrates, the faster yours does. It's a cycle that feeds on itself, lifting everyone higher and higher, toward ascension.

Gratitude boosts your career. People who show gratitude at their jobs are more likely to be promoted into higher positions with more responsibility. A leader who is grateful is much more effective than one who's a Debbie Downer. Think about it: Wouldn't you prefer to follow behind someone who is happy and grateful to be doing what they're doing? It's contagious. It makes you happy to be doing what you're doing!

Gratitude bolsters good emotions and weakens bad ones. The simple act of feeling grateful pushes energy and focus toward positive emotions. When you are practicing gratitude, the love you feel is more intense, stronger. And feelings like envy, fear, and desperation are tamped down and reduced.

Gratitude banishes materialism and other ego-based desires. When you are grateful for all your blessings and have a heart that is full, a message is sent out to The Universe that says you are ready for more amazing blessings to come your way. Gratitude creates more to be grateful for. And gratitude creates perspective—it allows you to see what really matters and where you should focus your love and energy. Gratitude is a form of love. When you give love, you get love in return. I have yet to see a purse, or a couch, or a pair of expensive shoes that offers unconditional love.

Gratitude connects you to The God Force. There is nothing self-centered about being grateful. In fact, gratitude is the opposite of self-centeredness: It connects you to all the good out there in the universe. When we dwell in the shadow side of our chakras, we deny the greatness and beauty God gave us. We deny the perfection with which God created each and every one of us. In being grateful, in feeling it and recognizing it, you are giving credit to God for creating all that is. You are raising your vibrations and becoming closer as one with The Divine. You are honoring the great and bountiful Universe. Focus on being thankful with the utmost sincerity, and you will quickly travel into your heart, where all goodness and blessings dwell.

SOUL KIT

Activate Your Light Body

In this Soul Kit I am asking you to surrender the unhealthy parts of your ego: the parts that are keeping you from the wonderful gifts that are yours for the taking. Our egos tell us the biggest lies and keep us from realizing our fullest potential. Try practicing the following techniques when your ego rears its ugly head.

1. **Let Go of Negative Emotions Through Forgiveness:** Think of a negative emotion (pride, anger, fear, jealousy) that is keeping you separate from what you truly enjoy. For example: Your father called you hurtful names when you were young, and you just can't seem to forgive him. Pride and anger are causing you to hold a grudge and are keeping you from attending family gatherings with people whose company you love and enjoy. Try to understand that at one time your father was a child too, and most likely an adult called him unfavorable names. He is only repeating a cycle that was created for him. Realize that people who are hurting usually hurt other people. This often makes them a perpetual bully. Do not take his name-calling personally; rather, try to find it in your heart to forgive and release the emotional baggage that is weighing you down. Practicing forgiveness and humility can work wonders in releasing the shadow side of our egos.

2. **Practice Gratitude Through the Law of Polarity:** We all know that what goes up must come down. Be grateful for every person and situation in your life— both the good and the bad. Every negative experience brings an opportunity to appreciate the positive when

it arrives. The Universe wants to provide us with every desire of our heart, but only if it is for the highest good of all concerned (balance). You may be on top of the world one day but fall flat on your face the next. Experience is the best teacher.

To practice gratitude, get out your journal and take five minutes to make a gratitude list. Think about all your blessings, big and small, good and bad, obvious and obscure. Here's one: Every time I walk down the street, I feel grateful that I have two working legs. And because I walk down a lot of streets, this one thing can keep me thankful throughout the day! After you've written your list, look back at whatever was making you feel bad earlier. Chances are, what you thought was a sticky situation, one in which you couldn't imagine a favorable outcome, is not half as bad as you thought.

3. **Have an Open Mind, Surrender, and Go with the Flow:** Ego has a tendency to make us believe it knows best in any given situation. Life is constantly sending us messages to release control and surrender to a higher wisdom. For example: Let's say you have your heart set on going to Mexico for an upcoming holiday. You research flights, only to see the prices are triple what you normally pay for the same trip. You look at the weather report for Mexico and see that the five-day forecast is calling for rain. You ignore it because you know that rain lasts for a shorter time there—you're prepared to take your chances.

Then you find out that your boss is going to be out of the office that same week, leaving no one to man the office. Your boss asks you if you can go to Mexico the following week, but you refuse. Your boss begins to view you differently, treating you with less respect—plus you wind up paying top dollar to fly to Mexico, and you come home with food poisoning. To top it all off, it rained the entire week of your trip. This became the worst vacation you had ever taken.

Never assume that you always know best. Next time, read the signs that are in front of you and surrender to the circumstances. When I need an answer from The Universe, I usually ask for three signs to point me in the right direction. In our hypothetical Mexico trip, the inflated airline prices was the first sign to stay home. The boss asking you to move your plans to the following week was the second sign. And the rainy forecast was the third sign. Understand that the big Eye in the Sky knows the outcome of every situation and has the best solution for all concerned.

Going through the ascension process is not as scary as it seems. The bottom line is our souls are aching to find new solutions to bring more peace and harmony into our lives. Remember, it is only when we get the call from The Universe to raise our vibrational frequencies that we will naturally move away from old habits, programs, and belief systems, which no longer serve us. As mentioned several times in this book, your soul already knows its purpose. The only thing left for you to do now is to try and keep rising higher and higher. When we operate through the center of our hearts, we send out a frequency that The Universe responds to immediately. It's like having a fast pass similar to the one you get at a theme park, allowing you priority entry to the exciting and fun ride. I truly believe that now that you have learned the many truths contained in this book, you cannot turn back. You have officially received your "wake-up call" from The Universe. Welcome Aboard!

Conclusion

Lastly, I want to relate to you the parable of the mustard seed, which appears in the Bible three times. It's one of Jesus's shortest parables. Here it is from the Gospel of Matthew: *The Kingdom of Heaven is like a grain of mustard seed, which a man took, and sowed in his field: which indeed is least of all seeds. But when it is grown, it is greater among herbs, and becomes a tree, so that the birds of the air come and lodge in its branches.*

Let me ask you: What is a mustard seed if it is not planted in the ground? When we live from day to day without passion, without purpose, we are like an unplanted mustard seed that's been swept up with the wind only to land in a cement parking lot with no purpose. But when the mustard seed is planted into the soil, it grows into something greater than just an herb. We are like the mustard seed. In order to flourish, we must take root in the Earth and become one with The Creator. Once we connect to the energy of the Earth, we will soar up with great beauty and power. We will live our purpose and our passion, reaching our fullest potential.

Not one of us is too insignificant to have an impact on the universe. Every one of us is made of atoms, the tiniest of building blocks, even smaller than a mustard seed. But with the right intentions, with our heart chakras open, we can raise the level of consciousness and the level of vibrations in the universe. We can turn away from greed and materialism toward the light, toward all that matters. We can be part of The God Force, with our hearts and minds open.

We will each, individually, be better for our efforts. And all the world will be better for our efforts.

By now, you've probably connected your soul purpose to your passion. Or perhaps your soul purpose has been circling around you for years trying to grab your attention. Either way, the good news is that it is never too late to answer the call from your soul. And surely you can see that passion can only come from your soul, which is your true self. The fact is: My soul purpose is connected to your soul purpose.

Let me explain: Throughout my life, I have been blessed with abundance from The Universe. I'm not referring to monetary blessings or physical gifts. I am referring to the knowledge and insight that was given to me by the people who passed through my life. These people have played an important role in my spiritual awakening. Some came to teach me, some came to challenge me, and some showed up just to love me. Their one commonality is that they all added meaning and purpose to my existence, they helped me evolve. What I have learned from these people has touched me deeply and inspired me to carry on in their spirit.

It is with love and gratitude that I have reached out to touch each one of you on your journey toward enlightenment and ascension. In writing this book, I have followed my passion, my soul purpose, which is to help you grow from the tiniest mustard seed into an all-loving, all-powerful body of light and energy. I can only hope that, in reading this book, you've found the beautiful, glowing light inside you—one that has always existed and was aching to come out and take the lead. I'm certain that once you've completed the work necessary to activate your light body, you've done it! You've banished the false selves within you, you've vibed with a community that reflects your Highest Self, and you've followed *your true passion* instead of following the expectations of others.

Simply put, you are connected with the only energy source that matters—the light within you. Once activated, this light will shine brightly for the world to see. It will brighten your darkest days and serve as a guide to bring you home to where your heart is. And this, my friend, is where you can find your soul purpose.

The light inside of me honors the light inside of you. As they say in the movies—*Up, up, and away!*

Namaste,
Kim Russo

Acknowledgments

It is said that everyone has a book inside of them. Truth be told, I have numerous books inside of me. But the very book that you are holding in your hand wasn't one of the books I thought I'd write at this point in time. This book came to me in a way that shocked even me. I know it's a bit strange for a psychic medium to say they were shocked, so let me explain:

As my fellow spiritual workers can attest, we sometimes don't pick up on information directed to ourselves as easily as we pick up on information directed to others. So, it was a complete surprise to me when during an unplanned encounter with the higher realms, I was told to write this book. Not *any* book, but *this book in particular*, with every chapter contained between the covers.

I am forever grateful to almighty God and to all of the souls who have been designated by God to guide and watch over me, especially Malick and Tuzeu: Thank you for entrusting me with your spiritual wisdom. It is a great honor and pleasure for me to serve as one of the chosen voices to share messages of love and truth in the form of this book.

I am also grateful to many people in the three-dimensional world, particularly the four amazing men in my life. First, to my amazing husband, Anthony: Thank you for your unwavering support, unconditional love, and endless sacrifices—especially during the writing of this book. I most appreciated it every time you checked in on me to see if I needed anything to eat. Thank God you did, because your delicious home-cooked meals kept me going for hours on end.

To my children, Nicholas, Joseph, and Anthony Jr.: Thank you for being my cheering section and for always encouraging me to follow my soul purpose. I am very proud of the men you have each become, and have no doubt that you are being divinely guided toward fulfilling your soul purposes.

I want to say a special thank you to my son Joseph, who designed and created the graphic images that appear inside of this book: Thank you for your great ideas and for dropping everything you were doing in order to accommodate meeting the deadlines that were in place. My love and appreciation for you extend beyond words.

To my mother—Maryann Scotti: Thank you for your love, encouragement, and for always believing in me. To my sister, Susan: Thank you for always having my back. You are my sister, my friend, and my confidante. To my brother, Neil: Thank you for always caring and for all of the laughter and love you bring to the world—you are one of a kind.

I could not have done this without my dream team at HarperOne, especially Lisa Sharkey, who approached me to write a second book for Harper around the same time as when Tuzeu imparted his valuable information to me. Whether or not Lisa realizes it, she too was picked by the higher realms to help facilitate the delivery of this vital information that will linger in the hearts of many throughout the ages. To you, Lisa: I am eternally grateful for all of your help and for following your soul purpose.

Getting a book ready for publication is a huge group effort; the following people each excelled in doing their part and I am forever thankful: Judith Curr, Anna Montague, Suzanne Wickham, Jennifer Jensen, Yvonne Chan, Terri Leonard, Laina Adler, Lisa Zuniga, Alieza Schvimer, and Alyssa Reuben.

To Jessica Blau: First and foremost, thank you for respecting my process of channeling spirit. I am very grateful that through your creative writing style and insight, not only were you able to help me capture the essence of spirits' teachings, but you were able to understand the importance of maintaining the clarity and purity of each message. I thank you, and my spirit guides thank you.

To my good friends Joann Wolff and Maria DeSimone: Thank you for taking time to consult on the astrology chapter of this book, and for checking in on my personal astrological chart whenever it's deemed necessary to continue to follow my soul purpose. You guys are the best astrologers under the sun, moon, and stars.

To my dear friend Stephanie Vriniotis: Thank you for sharing your extended knowledge of numerology and for just being you.

To Cristina Calvi of Monarch Photography: I admire your hard work and dedication to your craft. Thank you for taking so much time during our photoshoot. Who would have thought that one of those pictures would wind up on the cover of my new book? With your keen eyes and attention to detail, you are not only an outstanding photographer, you are a great person and I am proud to call you my dear friend.

To all of my sisters from other misters: I am beyond blessed to be amongst a special group of fierce spiritual warriors. I am in awe of the talents and endless dedication you exhibit to help raise the vibration of the collective consciousness. I am forever thankful to our special group for always creating a safe space where I can softly land when I'm having a bad day—a place that is free of judgment and filled with oodles and oodles of love and compassion. I wouldn't want to fly with any other Earth angels.

I am exceedingly grateful to all of my friends and clients who allowed me to share their stories in this book. You guys are true heroes. Your experiences will serve as meaningful examples to many who are seeking to find strength and inspiration.

To everyone else not mentioned here by name: If you are in my life in one way or another, it is very clear that we have agreed to share time and space, for a specific reason, during this Earthly go-around. Whatever value we bring to each other's lives, I know it has great meaning and purpose for the good of our collective souls—and for this I say thank you.

Lastly, I am grateful to you, my dear reader, for having the faith and courage to follow me on this very meaningful journey. I love you all.

About the Author

KIM RUSSO, known around the world as "The Happy Medium," is the author of *The Happy Medium* and starred on Lifetime Movie Network's popular shows *The Haunting Of . . .* and *Psychic Intervention*. One of the world's most sought after mediums, Russo's abilities as a highly evidential medium have been tested and verified by two highly respected organizations: The Windbridge Institute and The Forever Family Foundation, for which she serves on The Medium Advisory Board. Serving as a bridge between worlds, Russo considers herself to be a psychic journalist, priding herself in understanding the language of energy and carefully interviewing each spirit who is eager to connect with her. She is a repeat guest on many radio, news, and talk shows, including *The Doctor Oz Show*, *The Maury Povich Show*, and *The Real*. With her down-to-earth approach and compassionate heart, Russo is committed to her soul mission of helping to heal the hearts of many. She conducts readings, workshops, and lectures at hundreds of sold-out engagements across the country, addressing thousands of fans of different ages, religions, and beliefs. She currently lives in Long Island, New York.